3000
SYNONYMS
AND
ANTONYMS

Sam Phillips

GOODWILL PUBLISHING HOUSE
B-9, Rattan Jyoti, 18, Rajendra Place
New Delhi-110008 (INDIA)

Published by
Rajneesh Chowdhry
for
Goodwill Publishing House
B-9, Rattan Jyoti
18, Rajendra Place
New Delhi-110008
Tel. : 5750801, 5755519
Fax : 91-11-5763428

© Publisher

Typeset at
Radha Laserkraft
R-814, New Rajinder Nagar
New Delhi-110060 • Tel. : 5730031

Printed at
Kumar Offset Printers
Delhi-110031

Abandon
Syn. Discontinue, give up, leave, surrender, quit, forego.
Ant. Continue, carry on, keep, pursue, remain, chase, hunt.

Abandon
Syn. Imprudence, rashness, restlessness.
Ant. Prudence, care, thoughtfulness.

Abbreviate
Syn. Clip, condense, contract, shorten, trim.
Ant. Increase, expand, magnify, lengthen, stretch.

Ability
Syn. Capacity, capability, efficiency, competency, power qualification, skill, expertness, faculty, talented.
Ant. Incapacity, incapability, in efficiency, incompetence, unskilfulness, disqualification, impotency, unfitness, disability, inability.

Able
Syn. Capable, competent, skilful, efficient, learned, clever, talented.
Ant. Incapable, incompetent, unskilful, inefficient, unqualified, weak, impotent.

Abnormal
Syn. Unusual, irregular, unnatural, insane, peculiar, anamolous.
Ant. Usual, regular, natural, sane, ordinary methodical, normal.

Abode
Syn. Address, house, residence, dwelling, lodging, domicile.
Ant. Addresslessness, homelessness, foreignness.

1

Abolish
Syn. Destroy, cancel, suppress, extinguish.
Ant. Establish, confirm, support, encourage.

About
Syn. Approximately, roughly, nearly, almost.
Ant. Exactly, correctly, precisely, accurately, definitely.

Abridge
Syn. Shorten, condense, contract, diminish, reduce, lessen, compress, curtail.
Ant. Lengthen, expand, magnify, enlarge augment, extent, stretch, prolong.

Abound
Syn. Plentiful, teem, swarm.
Ant. Scarce, lack, want.

Absence
Syn. non-existence, non-presence, absenteeism, non-attendance, truancy.
Ant. Existence, presence, continuance, attendance.

Absolute
Syn. Unconditional, unlimited, complete, unrestricted, unmixed, perfect, entire, despotic, authoritative, imperative, autocratic, dictatorial.
Ant. Conditional, limited, incomplete, restricted, mixed, imperfect, relative, dependent, conditioned, servile.

Absolutely
Syn. Completely, entirely, totally, positively, definitely, indubitably.
Ant. In completely, partially, probably, possibly, perhaps.

Absolve
Syn. Acquit, discharge, excuse, exonerate, pardon.
Ant. Chastise, punish, penalize, castigate.

Absorb
Syn. Spend, waste, squander, burn, destroy, exhaust, devour, Assimilate.
Ant. Save, hoard, reserve, preserve, husband.

2

Abstain
Syn. Forbear, refrain, desist, withhold.
Ant. Pursue, adopt, persist, offer.

Abstract
Syn. Metaphysical, abstruse, theoretical, recondite.
Ant. Material, concrete, persist, offer.

Abundant
Syn. Lavish, ample, sufficient.
Ant. Scarce, limited, scanty, insufficient.

Abuse
Syn. Invective, contumely, obloquy, reproach, vituperation, misusage, opprobrium, scurrility.
Ant. Panegyric, praise, laudation, eulogy, economium, adulation, commendation, tribute.

Abuse
Syn. Vilify, slander, asperse, defame, calumniate, disparage, upbraid, malign, revile, traduce, vituperate.
Ant. Praise, exalt, applaud, glorify, laud, eulogize, panegyrize.

Accept
Syn. Approve, believe, take, assent, agree, honour, admit, confirm.
Ant. Disapprove, disbelieve, refuse, reject, disagree, non-consent.

Accident
Syn. Mishap, incident, chance, calamity, misadventure.
Ant. Design, purpose, intent, meaning, adventure

Accompany
Syn. Ascend, arise, climb, mount, rise, soar, tower, scale.
Ant. Descent, come down, dismount, fall, sink, alight, drop.

Accumulate
Syn. Asemble, gather, congregate, rally, board, store, convene.
Ant. Sprinkle, disperse, scatter, broadcast, spread, dissipate, sdistribute.

Accuse
Syn. Impeach, censure, charge, impute, blame, arraign, indict, tax, inculpate.
Ant. Ward, defend, protect, shelter, harbour, guard, shield.

3

Achieve

Syn. Attain, accomplish, do, win, effect, fulfil, gain, perform, finish, execute, acquire.

Ant. Fail, miss, miscarry.

Acknowledge

Syn. Own, avow, grant, concede, give, yield, admit.

Ant. Disown, disavow, deny, dispute, disclaim.

Across

Syn. Crosswise, athwart, transversely.

Ant. Beside, along, lengthwise, longitudinal, alongside.

Acquaintance

Syn. Friendship, knowledge, information, familiarity.

Ant. Enmity, ignorance, lack of knowledge, hostility.

Acquit

Syn. Excuse, clear, discharge, absolve, release, white wash liberate, pardon.

Ant. Accuse, charge, involve blame.

Act

Syn. Work, perform, imitate, show, display.

Ant. Laze, idle, hide, stand.

Active

Syn. quick, alert, busy, prompt, energetic.

Ant. Slow, dull, lazy, indolence, inactive.

Actual

Syn. Real, certain, existing, authentic, substantial, true, genuine, present.

Ant. Unreal, uncertain, potential, virtual, implied, tantamount.

Adapt

Syn. Fit, Regulate, conform, suit.

Ant. Misfit, irregularise, differ, disagree.

Address

Syn. Speak to, salute, hail, accost, court, woo, greet, appeal to.

Ant. Ignore, neglect, pass by, overlook, disregard, skip.

4

Adjust
Syn. Set in order, arrange, set right, regulate, accommodate, settle, set, compose.
Ant. Displace disarrange, dislocate, luxate, disconnect, derange, disjoin.

Admiration
Syn. Love, regard, respect, praise.
Ant. Hate, disregard, disapproval.

Admit
Syn. Own, avow, grant, concede, give, yield.
Ant. Disown, disavow, deny, dispute, disclaim.

Advance
Syn. Further, go, forward, progress, proceed.
Ant. Bend, go backward, regress, recede.

Advantage
Syn. Avail, utility, emolument, superiority, gain, profit, benefit, service.
Ant. Obstruction, hindrance, restraint, impediment, check.

Advantage
Syn. Benefit, service, emolument, gain, earnings, return.
Ant. Loss, detriment, forfeiture, deprivation.

Adversity
Syn. Affliction, misery, poverty, misfortune.
Ant. Prosperity, luck, fortune, happiness.

Advise
Syn. Warn, admonish, recommend, counsel, suggest, prompt.
Ant. Deter, dissuade, restrain, restrain, hinder, discourage, criticise.

Affecting
Syn. Touching, melting, moving, pathetic, eloquent, impressive.
Ant. Amusing, ludicrous, droll, ridiculous, absurd, funny, comic, laughable, farcical.

Affection
Syn. Love, devotion, fondness, tenderness, attachment, kindness, liking, passion, endearment, feeling.
Ant. Hate, indifference, coolness, coldness, negligence, carelessness, unconcern dislike, apathy.

Afraid

Syn. Frightened, scared, panicky, faint-hearted, anxious.
Ant. Brave, bold, courageous, unafraid, daring, upright.

Age

Syn. Date, time, period, epoch, era, generation.
Ant. Eternity, perpetuity, ceaselessness, endlessness.

Agent

Syn. Deputy, proxy, delegate, representative, substitute, factor, middleman.
Ant. Antagonist, opponent, competitor, opposer, rival.

Agony

Syn. Ache, woe, anguish.
Ant. Comfort, ease, peace, relief, enjoyment.

Agree

Syn. Conform, Coincide, tally, consent, concur, comply, accede.
Ant. Deviate, diverge, differ, vary, dissent, refuse, disagree, dispute.

Agreeable

Syn. Pleasant, acceptable, gratifying, pleasing, pleasurable, welcome, good, delicious.
Ant. Unpleasant, unacceptable, disgusting, hateful, objectionable, offensive, nasty.

Agreement

Syn. Consonance, harmony, unison, coincidence, concurrence, unanimity, accordance, concord.
Ant. Difference, disagreement, dissension, contention, variance, strife, discord, dispute.

Aid

Syn. Support, assistance, relief, contribute, relieve, co-operate, assist, support, help, befriend, succour.
Ant. Obstruction, check, hindrance, oppose, retard, hinder, obstruct, deter, impede.

Alarm

Syn. Frighten, startle, appal, terrify, intimidate.
Ant. Calm, compose, pacify, appease, still, quieten.

Alike
Syn. Similar, identical, equal, equivalent, resembling, same, allied.
Ant. Dissimilar, different, unlike, non-identical, diverse.

Allay
Syn. Lighten, abate, relieve, palliate, soothe, rid, assuage.
Ant. Aggregate, enhance, worsen, heighten.

Allow
Syn. Permit, authorise, yield, give, concede, admit, grant, sanction, apportion, assign, remit.
Ant. Renounce, deny, refuse, reject, disavow, abjure, refute, disclaim, abnegate, withhold, reserve.

Allure
Syn. Charm, invite, entice, draw, fascinate, endear.
Ant. Repulse, rebuff, reject, repel, deter, check.

Ally
Syn. Friend, accessory, abettor, agent, companion, cooperator, colleague, partner, accomplice.
Ant. Enemy, opponent, rival, competitor, opposer, foe, antagonist.

Almost
Syn. About, nearly, towards.
Ant. Precisely, exactly.

Always
Syn. Forever, ever, continually, everlastingly, perpetually, uniformly, constantly.
Ant. Never, at no time.

Amazing
Syn. Extraordinary, surprising, miraculous, marvellous, wonderous, stupendous, wonderful, astounding.
Ant. Ordinary, normal, common, everyday, commonplace, average, habitual, usual.

Ambition
Syn. Purpose, desire, wish, hope, intention, aspiration, ambition, goal, end.
Ant. Indifference, purposelessness, aimlessness.

Amongst
Syn. Amid, amidst, mid, between.
Ant. External, outside, outward, exterior.

Ample
Syn. Full, broad, unrestricted, unlimited, sufficient, large, spacious, abundant, extensive.
Ant. Scanty, short, restricted, limited, insufficient, small, skimpy, narrow.

Amuse
Syn. Please, enliven, entertain, gladden, charm, cheer.
Ant. Bore, annoy, tire, fatigue, vex.

Ancient
Syn. Antiquated, aged, old, hoary, antique, venerable.
Ant. Fashionable, new, young, modern, fresh, green.

Angle
Syn. Celestial being, seraph, cherub, ministering spirit.
Ant. Devil, demon, satan.

Anger
Syn. Resentment, rage, irritation, fury, annoyance, displease, vex, incite.
Ant. Calmness, peace, tranquillity, serenity, pacify, compose, reconcile.

Annexation
Syn. Increase, expansion, supplement, augmentation, accession, extension, appendix.
Ant. Decrease, contraction, curtailment, subtraction, diminution, reduction, fail.

Annihilate
Syn. Destroy, cancel, annual, suppress, extinguish, supersede, repeal.
Ant. Establish, confirm, support, encourage, promote, forward, produce, testify.

Announce
Syn. Declare, advertise, publish, reveal, notify, proclaim, promulgate.
Ant. Conceal, suppress, screen, withhold, cover-up, stifle, subdue.

Annoy
Syn. Worry, torment, trouble, vex, irritate, disturb, bother, harass, tease.
Ant. Please, charm, oblige, gratify, gladden, delight.

Annul
Syn. Destroy, cancel, suppress, repeal.
Ant. Establish, confirm, support, encourage.

Anxiety
Syn. Disquietude, apprehension, uneasiness, worry, misgiving, concern.
Ant. Quiet, assurance, ease, relief, tranquillity, peace, security.

Anxious
Syn. Concerned, troubled, solicitous, earnest, uneasy.
Ant. Careless, unmindful, negligent, heedless, thoughtless.

Apparent
Syn. Clear, visible obvious, evident, patent, manifest, distinct.
Ant. Hidden, obscure, obtruse, secret, covert, latent, masked, veiled.

Appearance
Syn. Phenomenon, sight, view, show, outlook, vista, scene, tableau, scenery, setting, picture, landscape.
Ant. Formlessness, disrespect, skeleton, insult.

Appetite
Syn. Ambition, desire, hunger, relish, craving, longing, gusto.
Ant. Realisation, contentment, satisfaction, apathy.

Appreciation
Syn. Love, regard, respect, praise.
Ant. Hate, disregard, disrespect, condemnation, disapproval.

Appropriate
Syn. Confiscate, take, allot, seize, correct.
Ant. Release, relinquish, open, loosen, incorrect.

Approve
Syn. Uphold, endorse, sanction, confirm, support, ratify, consent.
Ant. Correct, reprove, censure, admonish, condemn.

Argue

Syn. Debate, discuss, contend, dispute, reason, plead.

Ant. Concur, acquiesce, accede, assent, agree, consent.

Arrange

Syn. Put in, array, classify, dispose, group, adjust.

Ant. Separate, disarrange, scatter, disperse, diffuse, disseminate.

Arrest

Syn. Capture, detain, withhold, stop back, apprehend, obstruct, check.

Ant. Release, liberate, discharge, free, exempt, acquit, unloose.

Arrive

Syn. Attain, reach, come to land.

Ant. Depart, leave, decamp, vanish, withdraw, go.

Ascent

Syn. Further, go forward, progress, proceed.

Ant. Bend, go backward, progress, proceed.

Assent

Syn. Cheer, acclaim, clapping, admiration, praise.

Ant. Criticism, depreciation, jeers, censure, blame.

Assist

Syn. Support, assistance, relief, contribute.

Ant. Obstruction, check, hindrance, oppose.

Associate

Syn. Connect, ally, fraternise, join, combine, unite, relate, link.

Ant. Disconnect, separate, defy, part, dissociate, desert.

Assume

Syn. Pretend, affect, feign, sham, simulate, suppose, imply, presume, presuppose.

Ant. Abandon, cast off, discard, reprove, substantiate, confirm, establish, verify.

Astonish

Syn. Surprise, amaze, astound, startle, confound.

Ant. Forewarn, caution, warn.

Attach

Syn. Unite, link, join, conjoin, couple, combine.

Ant. Disunite, separate, cut, apart, sever, divide, part, detach, dissever.

Attempt

Syn. Enterprise, trial, essay, undertaking, experiment, effort, endeavour.

Attention

Syn. Regard, care, thoughtfulness, heed, mindfulness, concentration, note, notice.

Ant. Disregard, carelessness, neglect, heedlessness, negligence, inattention.

Attract

Syn. Allure, charm, invite, entice, draw, fascinate, captivate, endear.

Ant. repulse, rebuff, reject, repeal, deter, check.

Auspicious

Syn. Successful, hopeful, happy, fortunate, luck, proposition, reasonable.

Ant. Despairing, hopeless, unhappy, unfortunate, unlucky, luckless, ill-fated.

Authorise

Syn. Warrant, direct, sanction, empower, legalise, allow, permit.

Ant. Forbid, veto, prohibit, ban, proscribe.

Authority

Syn. Power, right, title, jurisdiction, influence, prestige, control, command, rule, sway.

Ant. Submission, obedience, subjection, thraldom, slavery.

Avoidance

Syn. Elusion, retreat, abstinence, evasion, the brush-off, the go by, escape, regression.

Ant. Continuation, firmness, status-quo, pursuit, discipline.

Awake

Syn. Alert, watchful, vigilant, ready, attentive.

Ant. Asleep, dormant, latent, slumbering, sleeping.

Awareness
Syn. Alertness, information, knowing, knowledge.
Ant. Carelessness, innocence, ignorance, foolishness.

Awkward
Syn. Unskilful, uncouth, ponderous, heavy-handed, rough, maladroit, bungling.
Ant. Skillful, dexterous, clever.

Backward
Syn. Unwilling, behind, dull, sluggish, late, tardy, reluctant, posterior.
Ant. Willing, ahead, anterior, quick, alert, early, advancing, forward, prompt, eager.

Bad
Syn. Defective, injurious, unsound, vile, hurtful, pernicious, corrupt, villainous, noxious, immoral, unprincipled, depraved, detrimental, deleterious, wicked.
Ant. Blameless, exemplary, good, honest, moral, harmless, wholesome, upright, virtuous.

Balance
Syn. Compensate, estimate, poise, equalise, weight, compare, neutralise.
Ant. Overbalance, invert, upset, subvert, overturn.

Bankrupt
Syn. Insolvent, penniless, ruined, indigent, destitute.
Ant. Solvent, credit-worthy, well-off, prosperous, rich, wealthy.

Bargain
Syn. Deal, inexpensivenes, transaction, agreement.
Ant. Account, closed, expensiveness, quittance, payment.

Baseless
Syn. False, groundless, unfounded, fanciful.
Ant. Real, substantial, existing, actual.

Basis
Syn. Bottom, foot, base, foundation, groundwork, support.
Ant. Top, summit, crown, apex, vortex, pinnacle, zenith.

Bear

Syn. Maintain, hold up, uphold, support, sustain, suffer, put up with, submit to, transport, carry, convey.

Ant. Leave, drop, discontinue, abandon, desert, resist, oppose, withstand, rebuff.

Beat

Syn. Throb, beating, pulsation, hit, batter, belabour, smite, strike, worst.

Ant. Kiss, caress, fondle, pat, embrace, hug.

Beauty

Syn. Loveliness, elegance, form, attractiveness, embellishment, fairness, glory, venus, grace, comeliness.

Ant. Unloveliness, inelegance, deformity, shapelessness, ugliness, ungainliness.

Before

Syn. Preceding, ahead of, prior to, in front of, previous to, formerly, above, already.

Ant. Succeeding, after, behind, later, following, subsequently, afterwards, later.

Beg

Syn. Crave, supplicate, appeal, implore, entreat.

Ant. Challenge, insist, contend, demand, claim.

Beginning

Syn. Start, opening, commencement, inception, origin, source, cause.

Ant. Close, end, expiration, conclusion, completion, finish, final.

Behaviour

Syn. Bearing, manner, carriage, conduct, department, demeanour, compartment.

Ant. Misconduct, misbehaviour.

Belief

Syn. Trust, credit, faith, opinion, idea, view, mind.

Ant. Distrust, whim, discredit, suspicion, doubt, disbelief, misgiving.

Below

Syn. Underneath, subordinate, under, beneath.

Ant. Overhead, over, above, aloft.

Bend

Syn. Incline, stop, bow, yield, submit, condescend, design, influence, bias, direct, subdue, swerve, curve, flex, deflect, deviate.

Ant. Straighten

Beneath

Syn. Below, underfoot, under, down.

Ant. Up, overhead, above, high.

Beneficial

Syn. Useful, advantageous, salutary, helpful.

Ant. Useless, wicked, wasteful, harmful.

Benefit

Syn. Advantage, gain, good, avail, profit, favour.

Ant. Disadvantage, loss, evil, damage, injury.

Benevolence

Syn. God's grace, selflessness, kindness, kindliness, charity, humanity, fellow-feeling,

Ant. Ill-nature, spite, cruelty, inhumanity, evil eye, intent, enmity, hate, malice, venom, churlishness, outrage.

Best

Syn. Precious, peerless, unequalled, choice, unparalleled.

Ant. Ordinary, most bad, humdrum, worst.

Between

Syn. Interjection, gatecrasher, partial, dovetailing, aside.

Ant. Externality, outsidedness, akin, outwardness, facet.

Bewilder

Syn. Problem poser, mystery, enigma.

Ant. Enlighten, teach, illuminate, inform, edify, instruct.

Beyond

Syn. Across, further, younder, farther, over.

Ant. Adjacent, beside, along, near, disallow.

Bid

Syn. Enjoin, order, offer, command, invite.

Ant. Deny, forbid, prohibit, refuse, disallow.

15

Big
Syn. Fat, enormous, great, large, bulky, huge, massive, important, weighty, impressive.

Ant. Thin, undersized, small, short, pigmy, little, kid.

Bind
Syn. Tie, fasten, connect, fetter, restrain, wrap, bandage.

Ant. Unite, undo, loosen, free, discharge, unfasten, liberate, unbind, unlock.

Binding
Syn. Obligatory, contracting, holding, restraining, stringent, valid.

Ant. Optional, voluntary, elective, discretional.

Birth
Syn. Origin, delivery, beginning, creation, genesis.

Ant. End, finish, close, death, conclusion.

Bit
Syn. Piece, slice, drill, cub, mite, sharp.

Ant. Complete, full, entire, total, whole.

Bitter
Syn. Sour, harsh, tart, acrid, acrimonious, sharp, cutting.

Ant. Sweet, nice, saccharine, genial, sugary, mellow, tasty, pleasant.

Black
Syn. Dark, dusty, cimmerian, ebon, inky, murky, dismal, sombre, gloomy.

Ant. Wane, pale, light, white, snowy, pallid, sparkling, sunny, bright, shining, luminous, glowing, brilliant, radiant.

Blame
Syn. Criticism, reproach, censure, guilt, rebuke.

Ant. Praise, appreciation, approval, exhort, applaud, extol.

Blend
Syn. Combine, mix, fuse, coalesce, amalgamate, unite.

Ant. Disconnect, separate, sever, disintegrate, scatter. disjoin, detach.

Blessings
Syn. Good wishes, prayer, thanks, praise, consecration.

Ant. Bad wishes, curse, evil thoughts.

16

Blind
Syn. Unseeing, sightless, eyeless, uninformed, unenlightened, ignorant, undiscerning.
Ant. Seeing, instructed, informed, educated, discerning enlightened.

Blindness
Syn. Sightlessness, darkness, stop, benightedness, cataract.
Ant. Slight, brightness, perfect, keenness of sight, sharpness.

Bliss
Syn. Joy, pleasure, happiness, rapture.
Ant. Sorrow, sadness, pain, dejection.

Blunt
Syn. Direct, insensitive, dull, undiplomatic.
Ant. Diplomatic, sensitive, sharp, sophisticated.

Boast
Syn. Moan, whine, shimper, snivel.
Ant. Vaunt, brag, bluster.

Body
Syn. Torso, structure, shape, matter, anatomy, person, substance, thing, whole.
Ant. Plan, idea, scheme, spirit, soul, ghost, phantom.

Bold
Syn. Fearless, brave, heroic, dauntless, doughty, valiant, intrepid, daring.
Ant. Afraid, cowardly, fearful, diffident, timid, timorous.

Boost
Syn. Encourage, aid, help, recommend, hoist, lift.
Ant. Discouragement, hinder, obstacle, rebuff, rebuke.

Bolder
Syn. Edge, brink, limit, hem, margin, boundary, brim, rim.
Ant. Centre, midst, point, middle, axis.

Bore
Syn. Troublesome, talker, nuisance, talkative, pest.
Ant. Thinker, genial, listener, entertainer, amusing.

17

Borrow

Syn. Receive, appropriate, take, adapt, adopt, steal, imitate, pilfer, pirate, copy.

Ant. Lend, advance, give, invent, improve, make, credit.

Bottom

Syn. Foot, base, sole, foundation, support.

Ant. Top, head, crown, turret, tip.

Boyhood

Syn. Youth, juvenility, adolescence, salad-days.

Ant. Old age, seniority, manhood, senility.

Boyish

Syn. Childish, youthful, juvenile, young.

Ant. Elderly, aged, antiquated, old.

Brace

Syn. Strengthen, invigorate, prop, support, refresh.

Ant. Weaken, degenerate, raze, knock, enfeeble.

Branch

Syn. Offshoot, shoot, limb, arm.

Ant. Root, stem, stock, stalk, trunk, body.

Branch

Syn. Department, sub-division, tributary, section

Ant. Whole, complete, oneness.

Branch

Syn. Deviate, diverge, ramify.

Ant. Approach, converge, come together, meet, incline.

Brave

Syn. Fearless, heroic, dauntless, doughty, valiant, intrepid, daring, bold.

Ant. Afraid, cowardly, fearful, diffident, timid, timorous.

Breadth

Syn. Broadness, width, extent, scope, bore, expanse, size, bulk.

Ant. Narrowness, length, tightness, smallness, undergrowth.

Break
Syn. Disobey, infringe, violate, destroy, shatter, fracture, burst, sever, split.
Ant. Obey, comply, submit, repair restore, join, mend, retouch, together.

Breed
Syn. Produce, raise, beget, conceive, train, hatch; incubate.
Ant. Destroy, slay, murder, annihilate, kill.

Breeze
Syn. Storm, gust, hurricane, wind, typhoon, blast, gale.
Ant. Calm, lull, placidity, doldrums.

Brevity
Syn. Shortness, conciseness, succinctness, briefness.
Ant. Confusedness, loquacity, muddle-headedness.

Brief
Syn. Condensed, compact, concise, short, curt, terse, transiern, fleeting transitory.
Ant. extended, detailed, lengthy, long, prolix, diffuse, prolonged, long, protracted.

Bright & Brilliant
Syn. Shining, quick-witted, intelligent, luminous, resplendent, sparkling.
Ant. Dull, dim, dull-witted, foolish, dark, ignorant, faint.

Brisk
Syn. Quick, alert, industrious, busy, lively, prompt, energetic.
Ant. Slow, dull, lethargic, lazy, indolent, inactive.

Broad
Syn. Capacious, spacious, ample, wide, vast, extensive.
Ant. Incapacious, limited, scanty, narrow, circumscribed, contracted.

Brusque
Syn. Discourteous, gruff, curt, abrupt.
Ant. Corteous, smooth, polite, polished.

Brutal
Syn. Inhuman, merciless, cruel, savage, pitiless, barbarous.
Ant. Humane, merciful, sympathetic, compassionate, kind, tender.

Build

Syn. Make, raise, erect, construct, fabricate.

Ant. Mar, demolish, overthrow, destroy, knock-down, rut, prostrate, raze.

Burial

Syn. Burying, inhumation, internment, entombment, sepulchre.

Ant. Disentombment, exhumation, disinternment.

Burn

Syn. Blaze, smoulder, flash, shrivel, glow, tan.

Ant. Extinguish, suffocate, stifle, asphyxiate, quench, smother.

Bury

Syn. Inearth, conceal, hide, entomb, inhume.

Ant. Unearth, disentomb, exhume, disinter.

Bustle

Syn. Rustle, fuster, flutter, stir, ado.

Ant. Intertness, laziness, lull, rest, unemployment, passivity, dullness, fatigue, delay, dawdling, dormancy, inaction.

Busy

Syn. Active, industrious, diligent, assiduous, employed, working, occupied, officious,, bustling, meddling, fussing.

Ant. Inactive, lazy, indolent, sluggish, slothfull, inert, idle.

Buy

Syn. Purchase, procure, acquire, corrupt, bribe.

Ant. Sell, retail, barter, peddle, hawk.

Cajole
Syn. Inveigle, beguile, coax, flatter, blandish, wheedle.
Ant. Cool, discourage, flout, dam, dissuade.

Calamity
Syn. Distress, misfortune, trouble, misery, catastrophe, affliction, disaster.
Ant. Prosperity, fortune, peace, joy, tranquillity, happiness.

Calculate
Syn. Reckon, count, assess, estimate, number, compute.
Ant. Imagine, conjecture, surmise, suppose.

Call
Syn. Bid, recall, invite, summon, muster, convene, convoke.
Ant. Remove, dismiss, discharge, exile, banish.

Calm
Syn. Pacify, hush, compose, quiet, solace, palliate, mitigate, lull.
Ant. Agitate, excite, perturb, trouble, disturb, fluster, crisis.

Cancel
Syn. Destroy, abolish, obliterate, blot out, efface, nullify, invalidate, erase, delete.
Ant. Establish, ratify, corroborate, substantiate, endorse, confirm.

Capacity
Syn. Capability, ability, competency, aptitude, faculty, skill, wit, talent, power.
Ant. Incapability, inability, incompetence, inaptitude.

Capture
Syn. Arrest, seize, snatch, catch, apprehend.
Ant. Liberate, release, acquit, free, disengage.

Care

Syn. Concern, solicitude, anxiety, custody, thrift.

Ant. Unconcern, coolness, coldness, apathy, indifference.

Care

Syn. Carefulness, regard, caution, attention, vigilance.

Ant. Unconcern, coolness, coldness, apathy, indifference.

Career

Syn. Progress, course, life, history, passage.

Ant Listlesness, uninterested, inattentive.

Careless

Syn. Thoughtless, improvident, inattentive, negligent, unmindful, heedless, neglectful.

Ant. Thoughtful, provident, attentive, vigilant, mindful, cautious, careful.

Caress

Syn. Pat, kiss, embrace, fondle.

Ant. Provoke, molest, torment, annoy.

Carry

Syn. Sustain, support, uphold,

Ant. Let fall.

Carry

Syn. Transfer, bear, convey, transport, haul, take.

Ant. Back, leave, desert, drop.

Casualty

Syn. Mishap, incident, chance, calamity, misadventure.

Ant. Design, purpose, intent, meaning, adventure.

Catching

Syn. Charming attractive, enchanting, captivating, winning, fascinating.

Ant. Unpleasant, ugly, unattractive, revolting, loathsome, repellent, odious, disagreeable.

Catching

Syn. Contagious, insidious, pestilential, infectious.

Cause
Syn. Produce, bring, abort, originate, evoke, create, effect.
Ant. Destroy, demolish, kill, devastate, ruin, desolate.

Caution
Syn. Carefulness, regard, cure, attention.
Ant. Carelessness, disregard, neglect, inattention.

Case
Syn. End, discontinue, stop, halt, pause.
Ant. Start, continue, begin, carry on, pursue.

Celebrated
Syn. Notable, distinguished, eminent, noted, illustrious
Ant. Unnoticed, undistinguished, unknown, unnoted nameless, obscure.

Celibacy
Syn. Single, singleness, bachelorhood, virginity, blessedness, maidenhood, chastity.
Ant. Engagement, wedlock, married state, matrimony, union, nuptial tie, intermarriage.

Censorship
Syn. Disapproval, criticism, blame.
Ant. Approval, commendation, appreciation, approbation.

Ceremony
Syn. Solemnity, formality, rite, display, observance, ceremonial.

Certain
Syn. Positive, definite, indisputable, sure, actual, unequivocal, incontestable.
Ant. Doubtful, indefinite, disputable, uncertain, ambiguous, equivocal, contestable.

Chaos
Syn. Disorder, confusion, jumble, abyss, void.
Ant. Order, organisation, government.

Character
Syn. Reputation, repute.
Ant. Discredit, disrepute.

Character
Syn. Mark, sign, emblem, figure, letter, symbol, temperament, nature, quality, constitution, disposition.

Ant. Indistinctive, derepute, without any style, unpreserved.

Charity
Syn. Kindness, benignity, generosity, phnanthropy, benevolence, beneficence, alms-giving, liberality.

Ant. Meanness, illiberality, greediness, selfshness.

Chase
Syn. Follow, hunt, pursue, track.

Ant. Forgo, renounce, withdraw, leave, abandon, forsake.

Cheap
Syn. Worthless, inferior, mean, paltry.

Ant. Worthy, superior, bob, honourable, eminent, expensive, dear, costly.

Cheat
Syn. Deceive, swindle, dupe, hoodwink, defraud. gyp, fleece, gull, hoax, bilk, delude.

Ant. Fairly play true, be above board, be just.

Check
Syn. Stop, restrain, hinder, control, curb, repress, subdue, impede.

Ant. Speed, hurry, expedite, accelerate, quicken, hasten, precipitate.

Cheek
Syn. Insolence, impertinence, effrontery, impudence, gall, nerve, brash.

Ant. Humility, politeness, gentleness, courtesy.

Cheer
Syn. Solace, comfort, gladden animate, enliven, console.

Ant. Deject, depress, dishearten, sadden, discourage, damp, condole.

Cheer
Syn. Applaud, clap, praise.

Ant. Decry, deprecate, disparage, vilify, condemn.

Chief
Syn. Premier, main, leading, supreme, cardinal, principal.
Ant. Petty, lesser, minor, inconsiderable, inferior, subordinate, junior, subsidiary.

Chief
Syn. Leader, head, captain, chieftain, principal, ruler, commander.
Ant. Follower, servant, dependent, parasite, minion.

Chill
Syn. Coldness, chilliness, shivering, shakes, frost, ague.
Ant. Warmth, fire, flame, glow, bonfire, fervour, fish.

Choice
Syn. Selection, option, alternative, adoption, preference.
Ant. Refusal, denial, rejection.

Choice
Syn. Precious, valuable, rare.
Ant. Cheap, inexpensive

Choice
Syn. Excellent, superior, select, exquisite.
Ant. Worthless, inferior, mean, indifferent.

Choke
Syn. Suffocate, strangle, smother, stifle, throttle.
Ant. Oxygenate freshen, ventilate, air.

Choose
Syn. Select, prefer, pick, elect, cull.
Ant. Reject, discard, renounce, spurn, disapprove.

Circulate
Syn. Propagate, spread, advertise, publish, diffuse, disseminate.
Ant. Quieten, silence, hush, supress.

Claim
Syn. Right, pretension, title, maintain, require, assume, challenge, demand.
Ant. Waive, drop, forgo, yield, renounce.

Class
Syn. Genus, division, kind, category, sort, degree, order, caste, grade.

25

Class
Syn. Arrange, distribute, group, rank, dispose, classify.
Ant. Disarrange, display, upset, disorder, confuse, derange.

Clean
Syn. Purify, clarify, cleanse.
Ant. Corrupt, infect, defile, soil, pollute, taint.

Clever
Syn. Talented, sharp, dexterous, capable, gifted, smart.
Ant. Foolish, dull, doltish, incapable, insensate, stupid.

Cling
Syn. Attack, adhere, stick, cleave, together, hold, clasp, embrace, hug.
Ant. Surrender, give up, forgo, relinquish, resign, cede.

Cloudy
Syn. Dark, dim, gloomy, murky, foggy, overcast.
Ant. Sunny, undimmed, unclouded, clear, bright, cloudless.

Clumsy
Syn. Unskilful, heavy-handed, rough.
Ant. Skilful, dexterous, clever.

Coarse
Syn. Unpolished, harsh, indelicate, unrefined, rude, gross.
Ant. Polished, polite, elegant, refined, civilised, genteel.

Coherence
Syn. Adherence, adhesion, adhesiveness, set, gel, jelly, cementation, stick, soldering, stickiness, density, gum, glue, gelatine, mire, mud, slush, syrup.
Ant. Isolation, disconnection, rupture, oasis, disunity, break, divorce, separateness.

Cold
Syn. Cool, chilly, wintry, icy, bleak, aretic, frosty, gelid.
Ant. Warm, hot, burning, boiling, tepid, oppressive, flaming.

Cold
Syn. Passionless, unfeeling, indifferent, unsympathetic, torpid, spiritless, unresponsive.
Ant. Passionate, ardent, fervent, fierce, fervid, impetuous, vehement, fiery.

Collect
Syn. Assemble, gather, rally, hoard, store.
Ant. Sprinkle, disperse, scatter, broadcast, spread, distribute.

Combat
Syn. War, battle, action, contest, broil, conflict.
Ant. Harmony, peace, concord, amity, agreement, quiet.

Combat
Syn. Strive, contend, battle, struggle, wrestle.
Ant. Coalsce, amalgamate, combine, unite.

Comfortable
Syn. Pleasant, agreeable, pleasing, convenient.
Ant. Irritating, disagreeable, displeasing, aggravating.

Comfortable
Syn. Satisfied, cosy, smug.
Ant. Distressed, disturbed, harassed.

Command
Syn. Commandment, order, direction, injunction, rule, behest, mandate, decree.
Ant. On liberty, free, approval, consent.

Command
Syn. Charge, order, direct, bid.
Ant. Comply, submit, obey.

Common
Syn. Low, vulgar, mean, lewd.
Ant. Refined, cultured, polished, genteel.

Common
Syn. Usual, frequent, ordinary, familiar, hackneyed, trite, general.
Ant. Unusual, infrequent, extraordinary, exceptional, unfamiliar, choice.

Companion
Syn. Friend, colleague, pal, comrade, shadow, accomplice, associate.
Ant. Enemy, rival, partisan.

Company
Syn. Collection, crowd, troupe, assemblage, group, gathering, firm, assembly, house, gang, conclave.
Ant. Individual.

Comparison
Syn. Similitude, illustration, simile.
Ant. Difference, contrariety, contrast.

Compassion
Syn. Kindness, tenderness, mercy, sympathy, condolence.
Ant. Cruelty, malignity, barbarity, savagery.

Compensation
Syn. Reparation, restoration, amends, recompense, restitution, atonement.
Ant. Injury, damage, hurt, detriment, wrong.

Compete
Syn. Contend, strive, rival, vie, emulate, contest.
Ant. Unite, combine, coalesce, amalgamate.

Competent
Syn. Capable, skilful, efficient, learned, clever, accomplished.
Ant. Incapable, unskilful, inefficient, unqualified, weak, incompetent.

Complete
Syn. Finished, perfect.
Ant. Unfinished, imperfect, incomplete.

Complete
Syn. End, finish, attain, consummate, fulfil, achieve,
Ant. Start, commence, originate, inaugurate, begin, institute.

Compulsory
Syn. Necessary, unavoidable, binding, imperative, obligatory.
Ant. Voluntary, avoidable, optional, unconstrained.

Compliment
Syn. Praise, congratulate, flatter, commend.
Ant. Criticism, censure, disapprobation.

Compromise
Syn. Settlement, concession, compensation, commutation, mediation.
Ant. Hard-headedness, resolution, obstinacy, wilfulness.

Conceit
Syn. Self-esteem, caprice, pride, fantasy.
Ant. Timidity, nervousness, shamefacedness, unpretentiousness, diffidence, reserve, constraint, humility.

Concerning
Syn. About, respecting, anent, with regard to, regarding, with reference to.
Ant. Indifferent, unconcerned, not related to, neutral.

Conclusion
Syn. End, completion, issue, inference, result, close, upshot, deduction.
Ant. Beginning, opening, inception, commencement, origin, start.

Condemn
Syn. Sentence, doom, convict.
Ant. Liberate, clear, acquit discharge, exonerate, exculpate.

Condemn
Syn. Blame, denounce, censure, reproach.
Ant. Praise, flatter, compliment, exalt.

Condense
Syn. Shorten, summarise, abridge, epitomise.
Ant. Expand, enlarge, augment, amplify.

Condense
Syn. Contract, squeeze, reduce, compress, concentrate.
Ant. Hotch-potch, confused, disorganised.

Condition
Syn. Stipulation, consideration, covenant, term, state, situation, case, circumstance, plight.
Ant. Unfit-state, unconditional, comprehensive.

Conduct
Syn. Bearing, deportment, demeanour, behaviour, manner, actions.
Ant. Misbehaviour, misconduct.

Conduct
Syn. Direct, guide, lead, escort, control, convoy, transit.
Ant. Misdirect, misguide, mislead, deceive, delude, conceit.

Confess
Syn. Admit, own, disclose, concede, acknowledge.
Ant. Deny, disown, renounce, refute, disclaim abjure.

Confidence
Syn. Trust, hope, faith, assurance, reliance.
Ant. Distrust, suspicion. doubt, unbelief, discredit, dubiety.

Confirm
Syn. Countersign, verify, ratify, substantiate, strengthen, endorse, corroborate, fix.
Ant. Countermand, invalidate, cancel, annul, confute, repeal, deny.

Conflicting
Syn. Interfering, discordant, opposite, irreconciliable, jarring.
Ant. Agreeing, corresponding, matching, coinciding, harmonizing, harmonious.

Confuse
Syn. Discompose, embarrass, abash, disconcert.
Ant. Compose, reassure, appease, encourage.

Confuse
Syn. Disorder, confound, mingle, mystify, astound.
Ant. Arrange, group, classify, clarify, instruct, clear, enlighten, illuminate.

Connect
Syn. Unite, link, join, conjoin, couple, combine.
Ant. Disunite, separate, cut, apart divide, part, detach.

Connection
Syn. Association, junction, union, alliance.
Ant. Separation, disjunction, disunion, severance, parting.

Connection
Syn. Relation, affinity, relationship, kinsman, relative, kindered.
Ant. Unconcerned, not related to, parted, separated.

Conquer
Syn. Defeat, overthrow, subjugate, prevail over, overpower, surmount, overcome.
Ant. Surrender, forgo, abandon, renounce, yield.

Conscientious
Syn. Uncorrupt, principled, faithful, straightforward, honourable.
Ant. Corrupt, profligate, wicked, vile.

Consequence
Syn. Result, issue, outcome.
Ant. Cause, origin, source, ground, reason.

Consequence
Syn. Achieve, carry out, consummate, accomplish.
Ant. Fail, miscarry, overlook, neglect.

Considerate
Syn. Thoughtful, attentive, heedful, circumspect, king.
Ant. Thoughtless, inattentive, heedless, negligent, unconcerned.

Consistency
Syn. Harmony, compatibility, coherence, accordance, congruity, consonance, uniformity.
Ant. Disharmony, incompatibility, discord, inconsistency.

Constant
Syn. Steady, firm, unswerving, steadfast.
Ant. Unsteady, changeable, variable, inconstant, unreliable, unstable, fickle.

Constant
Syn. Perpetual, continuous, unbroken, sustained, incessant.
Ant. Discontinuous, intermittent, recurrent, spasmodic, periodic.

Construct
Syn. Make, raise, erect, fabricate.
Ant. Mar, demolish, overthrow, destroy, knock-down, gut, prostrate.

Consult
Syn. Question, interrogate, confer, deliberate, bebate, ask.
Ant. Avoid, uncare, unheed.

Consultation
Syn. Discussion, meeting, confer, deliberate, debate, deliberation, colloquy.
Ant. Inhibition.

Consume
Syn. Spend, waste, burn, destroy, exhaust.
Ant. Save, hoard, reserve, preserve.

Consumption
Syn. Extinction, decline, waste, expenditure, dissipation, destruction.
Ant. Savings.

Contempt
Syn. Lovelessness, dislike, slight, disregard, hate, sneer, cold, shoulder, hoot, cat-call.
Ant. Love, respect, good-heartedness, regard, fellow feeling, reverence.

Contentment
Syn. Satisfaction, pleasure, contentedness, appeasement, happiness, comfort.
Ant. Dissatisfaction, displeasure, discontent, bitterness.

Continuity
Syn. Succession, round, suite, progression, series, train, chain, perpetuity, scale, gradation, procession, column, retinue, caravan, rank and file, running fire, tier, lineage.
Ant. Isolation, disconnection, disunion, rupture, oasis, disunity.

Contract
Syn. Bargain, convention, compact, stipulation, convenant, bond, treaty, undertaking.
Ant. Unacceptable.

Contradict
Syn. Gainsay, refute, disprove, contravene, deny, confute.
Ant. Endorse, ratify, corroborate, substantiate, confirm, avouch.

Contrary
Syn. Hostile, antagonistic, adverse, counteracting, contradictory.
Ant. Favourable, advantageous, friendly.

Control
Syn. Quell, check, subdue, regulate, hinder.
Ant. Free, relieve, liberate, disengage, release, unbind.

Controversy
Syn. Dispute, argument, contention, bickering, debate, disputation.
Ant. Agreement, compromise.

32

Convenient
Syn. Suitable, comfortable, adapted, handy, advantageous.
Ant. Unhand, inconvenient, cumbersome.

Convenient
Syn. Suitable, proper, fit, appropriate.
Ant. Unsuitable, improper, unfit, inappropriate, unbecoming.

Co-operation
Syn. Unity, participation, unison, fellowship, uniformity, fusion alliance, masonry, union, logrolling.
Ant. Enmity, heads and tails, inversion, rivalry, counterplot, dislike, hate, clashing, restraint, contradiction.

Copy
Syn. Imitation, transcription, duplicate, transcript, facsimile.
Ant. Original one, genuine, actual.

Copy
Syn. Reproduce, duplicate, transcribe, portray, imitate, trace.
Ant. Initiate, originate, create.

Correct
Syn. Accurate, true, precise, proper, exact, right.
Ant. Inaccurate, wrong, erroneous, incorrect, false.

Correct
Syn. Reform, rectify, redress, mend, improve.
Ant. Damage, impair, injure, spoil, harm.

Correct
Syn. Discipline, punish, chastise.
Ant. Indulge, gratify, satisfy, pamper.

Correspond
Syn. Agreement, similarity, correlation, match, concurrence.
Ant. Disagreement, variance, difference, jarring, dissonance.

Correspondence
Syn. Communication, letters, despatches.
Ant. Separation, untouched, parted, disunion.

33

Corruption
Syn. Adulteration, vileness, putrescence, debasement, contamination, putrefaction.
Ant. Pure, unadulterated.

Costly
Syn. Dear, high-priced, expensive, valuable.
Ant. Cheap, low-priced, inexpensive, inferior.

Count
Syn. Reckon, assess, estimate, number, compute.
Ant. Imagine, conject, suppose, guess, surmise.

Country
Syn. Kingdom, dominion, province, state, empire, realm, motherland.
Ant. Eternal, everlasting, ceaseless.

Courage
Syn. Bravery, boldness, heroism, interpidity, valour, mettle.
Ant. Cowardice, timidity, diffidence, pusillanimity.

Cowardice
Syn. Fear, cowardliness, timidity, baseness, faint-heart, whiteliar.
Ant. Boldness, bravery, courage, heroism.

Cover
Syn. Hide, screen shield, veil, protect, mask.
Ant. Decry, denounce, expose, unveil, uncover, exhibit, bare.

Create
Syn. Produce, form, fashion, engender, generate, originate.
Ant. Destroy, devastate, kill, annihilate, extirpate.

Credit
Syn. Belief, confidence, trust worthiness, faith, trust, reliance.
Ant. Disbelief, mistrust, suspicion, misgiving, distrust.

Credit
Syn. Honour, praise, merit.
Ant. Censure, blame.

Crime
Syn. Evil, wrong-doing, offence, outrage, guilt.
Ant. Modesty, incorruption, guiltlessness, blamelessness, alertness.

Critic
Syn. Reviewer, connoisseur, commentator, censor, expert, judge.
Ant. Appreciator, spectator, reader, student, professor.

Crowd
Syn. Throng, swarm, assemblage, flock, mob, rabble.
Ant. Select, chosen, elite.

Crude
Syn. Rough, coarse, unfinished, immature, undigested, raw.
Ant. Fine, smooth, finished, mature, perfect, elegant.

Cruel
Syn. Inhuman, merciless, unfeeling, inexorable, callous, pitiless.
Ant. Human, merciful, sympathetic, tender, kind, compassionate.

Crush
Syn. Pulverise, confuse, triturate, power, squeeze, compress.
Ant. Solidify, weld, harden, congregate, consolidate, fuse.

Crush
Syn. Overcome, suppress, subdue, overpower, overwhelm.
Ant. Save, empower, aid.

Cry
Syn. Weeping, crying, lamentation, lament, plaint, slogan, scream. howl, exclamation.
Ant. Laughter, revelry, exultation, joy, silence, speechlessness.

Cry.
Syn. Weep, lament, sob, bawl, scream, exclaim, shriek, publish, proclaim, blazon.
Ant. Revel, rejoice, glory, exalt.

Cure
Syn. Specific, alleviation, remedy, antidote, restorative, corrective.
Ant. Heightening, aggravation, worsening.

Cure
Syn. Heal, remedy, restore.
Ant. Aggravate, worsen, increase, heighten.

Curiosity
Syn. Interest, inquisitiveness.
Ant. Indifference.

Curse
Syn. Imprecation, malediction, anathema, bane, execration.
Ant. Benediction, thanksgiving, blessing.

Cutting
Syn. Biting, provoking, trenchant, piercing, sharp, satirical.
Ant. Soothing, Flattering, commendatory, complimentary.

Cynical
Syn. Carping, censorious, testy, snappish, sophisticated, captious.
Ant. Charming, complimentary, amiable, engaging, appreciative.

Dainty
Syn. Elegant, refined, delicate, fine, exquisite, fastidious.
Ant. Inelegant, vulgar, indelicate, rough, coarse, un-polished.

Damage
Syn. Loss, injury, detriment, hurt.
Ant. Indemnify, atonement, compensation, redress.

Damage
Syn. Mar, disfigure, deface, hurt.
Ant. Mend, restore, repair, renovate.

Danger
Syn. Insecurity, risk, hazard, jeopardy.
Ant. Security, protection, safety.

Dark
Syn. Black, swarthy, dusky, sable, ebony.
Ant. White, snowy, whitish, bright.

Dark
Syn. Shadowy, cloudy, unilluminated, dim, sunless.
Ant. Light, clear, illuminated, bright, luminous.

Dark
Syn. Hidden, secret, obscure, mystic, abstruse.
Ant. Clear, open, evident, unmistakable, simple.

Dead
Syn. Departed, deceased, past, gone.
Ant. Living, breathing, alive.

Dead
Syn. Inanimate, unconscious, lifeless, inert, unfeeling, heavy.
Ant. Animated, conscious, lively brisk, exciting, thrilling, stirring.

Death
Syn. End, demise, dissolution, mortality, exit, expiration.
Ant. Start, birth, beginning, source, nativity.

Debate
Syn. Discuss, contend, dispute, reason, plead.
Ant. Concur, acquiesce, accede, assent, agree, consent.

Decay
Syn. Deterioration, sinking, decline, wearing, degeneracy, fail.
Ant. Improvement, progress, expansion, development, enlargement.

Decay
Syn. Perish, rot, decompose, wither.
Ant. Flourish, grow, develop, progress, prosper.

Decide
Syn. Settle, determine, conclude, adjudicate, resolve.
Ant. Drop, falter, dubitate, waive, waver.

Decision
Syn. Determination, conclusion, resolution, judgement.
Ant. Ambiguity, uncertainty.

Decline
Syn. Determination, conclusion, resolution, decay, decrease.
Ant. Improvement, progress, increase.

Decline
Syn. Reject, refuse, discard, renounce, waste, sink, degenerate. decrease, lessen, fall, droop.
Ant. Accept, accede to, agree to, admit, grow, aggravate, enhance, increase.

Decrease
Syn. Reduce, decline, subside, diminish, lessen.
Ant. Increase, enlarge, enhance, extend, augment, advance, intensify.

Deed
Syn. Action, feat, exploit, work, victory, achievement.
Ant. Inertness, restful, unemployment, passivity, dullnes, fatigue, dawdling, dormancy, delay.

Defence
Syn. Protection, shelter, guard, dike, ditch, breast-work, screen, earthwork.
Ant. Transgression, aggression, attack, crime, disgrace, discourtesy.

Defeat
Syn. Overcome, rout, outwit, frustration, foil.
Ant. Prevail, triumph, win, overthrow, vanquish.

Defect
Syn. Fault, flaw, spot, imperfection, blemish.
Ant. Faultless, flawless, spotlessness, perfection, excellence.

Defend
Syn. Protect, shelter, shield, guard, justify, exonerate, support.
Ant. Attack, charge, invade, contavene, censure, blame, reprehend, reprimand, condemn.

Degree
Syn. Space, interval, division, class, station, grade, position, rank, order, standing.
Ant. Undivided, ungraded, unrated.

Delicacy
Syn. Smoothness, softness, nicety, refinement, lightness, slenderness, elegance.
Ant. Roughness, inelegance, hardiness, robustness, crudeness, heaviness.

Delicious
Syn. Pleasant, pleasure, bliss, joy, ravishment.
Ant. Unhappiness, sadness, suffering, misery, anguish, grief.

Deliver
Syn. Free, discharge, liberate, surrender, release, rescue, save, consign, cede, yield, relinquish, commit, hand over.
Ant. Arrest, imprison, capture, apprehend, catch, seize, adopt, withhold, keep, appropriation.

Democracy
Syn. Republic, popular, non-snobbishness, rule of the people.
Ant. Dictatorship, mobocracy, aristocracy, despotism, autocracy.

Denote
Syn. Signify, mark, mean, imply, indicate, designate.
Ant. Dissemble, suppress, conceal.

Deny
Syn. Reject, withhold, refute, controvert, disclaim, contradict, renounce, abjure.
Ant. Confirm, comply, ratify, verify, endorse, acknowledge, substantiate.

Depart
Syn. Decamp, leave, retire, quit, disappear, go, vanish, withdraw.
Ant. Land, come, arrive, reach.

Department
Syn. Section, function, division, office, province, branch, station.
Ant. Undivided, whole, not broken, complete, unzoned.

Dependence
Syn. Slavery, helplessness, thraldom, reliance.
Ant. Delivery, permission, licence, independence, discharge, play, latitude, release, free, trade, swing, full scope.

Dependent
Syn. Hanging, relying, pendant, conditioned.
Ant. Autonomous, unrestricted, independent, unfettered.

Describe
Syn. Explain, relate, illustrate, tell, draw, picture, define, narrate, recount.
Ant. Falsify, mystify, misrepresent, suppress, obscure, misinterpret.

Description
Syn. Statement, rectal, delineation, narration, account, report, portrayal.
Ant. Suppression, misinteruption, unacquainted, inexplicably.

Design
Syn. Outline, drawing, scheme, painting, plant, project, purpose, intention, contrive, scheme, plot, prepare, devise.
Ant. Hotch-potch, plain, unplanned, unintentioned.

Desirable
Syn. Delightful, advisable, beneficial, enviable, profitable, valuable.
Ant. Hateful, disgusting, abhorrent, abominable, odious, detestable.

Desire

Syn. Passion, craving, eagerness, proclivity, lust, longing.

Ant. Aversion, loathing, hatred, repugnance, dislike, distaste, disgust.

Desire

Syn. Yearn for, covet, hanker after, lust, want, crave, long for, wish for.

Ant. Detest, despise, hate, loathe.

Despair

Syn. Sadness, dejection, discouragement.

Ant. Good humour, life, vivacity, sunsiness, lightheart, optimism, animation, playfulness, mirth, peace of mind.

Destiny

Syn. Destination, future, decree, doom, end, fate, lot, fortune.

Ant. Beginning, present, undesigned, unpurposed.

Destroy

Syn. Wither, ravage, eradicate, kill, shrivel, extripate, subvert, demolish, blast, exterminate, uproot.

Ant. Rootage, rooted, non-execution, ueutralisation.

Destruction

Syn. Devastation, demolition, desolation, annihilation, subversion.

Ant. Creation, production, formation, making.

Determination

Syn. Constancy, steadiness, firmness, fixity, persistence, resoluteness, fortitude.

Ant. Inconstancy, irresolution, unsteadiness, weakness, vacillation.

Deviate

Syn. Diverge, swerve, stray, ramble, wander, err, vary, charge, differ.

Ant. Converge, stay, perpetuate, continue, persist, abide.

Devil

Syn. Satan, demon, wretch, fiend, unfortunate.

Ant. Celestial being, seraph, ministering spirit, cherub.

Devoted

Syn. Affectionate, assiduous, dedicated, fond, loving, ardent.

Ant. Unfaithful, faithless, indifferent, cool, disloyal.

Devotion
Syn. Liking, love, attachment, affection, ardour.
Ant. Dislike, hate, hatred, abhorrence, detestation, antipathy.

Devotion
Syn. Piety, worship, holiness, adoration, devoutness.
Ant. Profanity, blasphemy, irreverence, sacrilege.

Difference
Syn. Distinction, dissimilarity, disparity, divergence, disagreement, discord, contention, dissent, strife.
Ant. Uniformity, harmony, similarity, convergence, agreement, accord, obligation, compact, bond.

Difficulty
Syn. Hardness, tough job, Herculean task, horns of dilemma, coil mice point, maze, mess, bone to pick.
Ant. Easiness, smoothness, smooth, pliancy, snap, clinch, sinecure, flexibility, capability.

Digest
Syn. Arrange, classify, systematise, tabulate, consider, study, assimilate, master, reflect.
Ant. Disarrange, confuse, disorder, unsettle, ignore, neglect, disregard, derange.

Diligent
Syn. Careful, laborious, attentive, busy, painstaking.
Ant. Slack lazy, indolent, idle, slothful.

Dimension
Syn. Extent, magnitude, capacity, bulk, size, mass, measurement, volume.
Ant. Eternal, unlimited, unmeasured, unscrolled.

Diminish
Syn. Curtail, decrease, lessen, contract, abate, subside.
Ant. Advance, increase, multiply, augment, intensify.

Diplomacy
Syn. Circumvention, strategy, tact, tactics.
Ant. Imprudence, blunder, indiscretion.

Diplomatic
Syn. Discreet, prudent, sagacious, judicious, astute, sharp shrewd.
Ant. Indiscreet, imprudent, untactful, injudicious, silly, bungling.

Dirty
Syn. Unclean, impure, dingy, sullied, squalid, filthy, grimy.
Ant. Clean, pure, unsullied, unsoiled, spotless, immaculate.

Disappear
Syn. Vanish, fade away, cease, dissolve, melt away, recede.
Ant. Appear, open, arrive, dawn, emerge.

Disappointment
Syn. Gloominess, sadness, let down, frustration, chagrin, failure.
Ant. Good humour, life, vivacity, sunniness, jollity, playfulness, peace of mind, with mirth, glee.

Disclose
Syn. Reveal, uncover, confess, expose, unveil, betray, discover, unfold.
Ant. Conceal, covert, suppress, hide, veil, dissemble, cloak.

Discontent
Syn. Dissatisfaction, soreness, fool's paradise, mirage, blow, vain expectation, blighted hope.
Ant. good, humour, life, peace of mind, glee.

Discretion
Syn. Prudence, carefulness, caution, wariness, judiciousness, care.
Ant. Imprudence, recklessness, foolhardiness, heedlessness, indiscretion, blind, bargain, scape-grace, gambling.

Discuss
Syn. Argue, debate, contend, examine, dispute, deliberate, reason.
Ant. Agree, concur, acquiesce, consent, assent, accede.

Disease
Syn. Ailment, sickness, disorder, indisposition, infirmity, complain.
Ant. Health, soundness.

Disgrace
Syn. Dishonour, shame, degrade, discredit, disparage, humiliate.
Ant. Honour, reverence, respect, exalt, dignify, elevate, venerate.

Disgrace
Syn. Scandal, odium, obloquy, ingominy, discredit, reproach.
Ant. Esteemed, reputable, famous, deem.

Disgust
Syn. Dislike, abhorrence, detestation, repugnance, aversion, loathing, nausea.
Ant. Liking, fondness, appreciation, employment, zest, gusto, relish.

Disgust
Syn. Displease, sicken, nauseate, offend, repulse.
Ant. Please, rejoice, delight, gratify, charm, gladden.

Dishonest
Syn. Deceitful, deceptive, fraudulent, crooked, tricky, treacherous, false.
Ant. Honest, fair, reliable, straightforward, trustworthy, just.

Displace
Syn. Dislocate, remove, oust, supplant, supersede.
Ant. Establish, settle, set, secure, root, plant.

Dispute
Syn. Discuss, bicker, brawl, wrangle, argue, quarrel.
Ant. Assent, consent, comply, agree, accede.

Dispute
Syn. Controversy, discussion, fight, bickering, debate, contention, alteraction, brawl, quarrel.
Ant. Harmony, compact, agreement, amiability, cordiality, understanding.

Dissolve
Syn. Disunite, divide, separate, break up, disperse, part, disconnect.
Ant. Unite, combine, concert, join, conjoin, amalgamate, connect.

Distinguished
Syn. Notable, eminent, noted, famed, illustrious.
Ant. Unnoticed, obscure, unknown, unnoted, nameless

Disturb
Syn. Disarrange, unsettle, derange, upset, confuse, interrupt, annoy, harass, trouble, worry, shake.
Ant. Arrange, group, distribute, assert, classify, placate, soothe, conciliate, appease, pacify.

44

Divide

Syn. Disunite, disconnect, part, separate, cleave, sever.
Ant. Unit, connect, join, combine, amalgamate, link.

Divide

Syn. Alienate, estrange.
Ant. Unite, bring together.

Divide

Syn. Dispense, distribute, deal out, share.
Ant. Assemble, collect, amass, collate, gather, glean.

Divorce

Syn. Divorcement, annulment, separation, grass-widow.
Ant. Engagement, wedlock, married, matrimony, union, nuptial, inter-marriage, sea of matrimony.

Down

Syn. Low, blow, beneath, prostrate, fur, feathers.
Ant. High, above, up.

Dramatic

Syn. Sensational, Thespian, melodramatic, theatrical, histrionic, showy.
Ant. Unsensational, drab, simple, prosaic.

Draw

Syn. Allure, entice, attract, haul, pull, tow, tug, depict, describe, sketch.
Ant. Distract, perplex, confusion, detatchment.

Dreadful

Syn. Frightful, alarming, horrible, awful, dire, fearful, terrific.
Ant. Pleasing, pleasurable, propitious, reassuring, auspicious.

Dream

Syn. Reverie, fantasy, vision, fancy, delusion, nightmare, hallucination.
Ant. Reality, practicality, materiality, embodiment.

Drink

Syn. Absorb, imbibe, swallow, quaff, sip.
Ant. Discard, throwout, discharge, excrete.

Drive
Syn. Push, press, forward, urge on, propel, force along, impel.
Ant. Pull, draw, drag, haul, tug.

Drunk
Syn. Tipsy, inebriated, muddled, intoxicated, fuddled.
Ant. Abstinent, abstemious, humid, damp, wet.

Dry
Syn. Uninteresting, dull, vapid, boring, tiresome, tedious.
Ant. Interesting, lively, gay, enthralling, jolly.

Dry
Syn. Thirsty, parched, arid.
Ant. Soaked, drenched, humid, damp, wet, satiated.

Due
Syn. Becoming, appropriate, proper, fair fit, owing, obligatory.
Ant. Unbecoming, inappropriate, inadequate, deficient.

Dull
Syn. Foolish, uniteresting, stupid, stolid.
Ant. Wise, intelligent, clever, talented.

Dull
Syn. Gloomy, cheerless, sad, dismal.
Ant. Jolly, merry, cheerful, gay, joyful, joyous

Dull
Syn. Monotonous, uninteresting, tiresome, boring, dreary.
Ant. Interesting , spirited, enthralling, lively.

Duty
Syn. Tax, toll, excise, impost, tariff, custom, responsibility, obligation, business, trust.
Ant. Leisure, free, annex, addititious, right.

Eager
Syn. Excited, anxious, fervent, impatient, zealous, enthusiastic, keen.
Ant. Cool, unconcerned, indifferent, apathetic, loath, disinterested.

Early
Syn. Soon, premature, quickly, ere long, anon.
Ant. Late, overdue, tardy, slow, delayed.

Earn
Syn. Win, achieve, gain, obtain, acquire, deserve, merit.
Ant. Lose, forgo forfeit, alienate, renounce.

Economical
Syn. Careful, provident, thrifty, sparing, frugal, saving.
Ant. Spend-thrift, improvident, extravagant, liberal, prodigal.

Educate
Syn. Discipline, instruct, train, nurture, teach, rear.
Ant. Neglect, mislead.

Effect
Syn. Result, issue, outcome.
Ant. Cause, origin, source, ground, reason.

Effective
Syn. Efficient, efficacious, potent, active, powerful.
Ant. Inefficient, ineffectual, futile, useless, fruitless, worthless, unavailing.

Efficiency
Syn. Potency, capability, competency, efficacy, virtue, effectiveness.
Ant. Impotency, incapability, futileness, inefficiency.

Embrace
Syn. Include, incorporate, contain, comprehend, embody, enclose, encircle.
Ant. Exclude, veto, except, bar, ban, preclude, debar.

Enchanted
Syn. Fascinated, bewitched, captivated, enraptured, enamoured, entranced, spell-bound, charmed.
Ant. Disgusted, repulsed, repeled, nauseated.

Encircle
Syn. Embrace, begird, surround, hem in, encompass.
Ant. Except, reject, exclude, preclude.

Endanger
Syn. Hazard, venture, jeopardise, risk, imperil.
Ant. Protect, safeguard, shield, defend, screen.

Endless
Syn. Unlimited, limitless, infinite, interminable, continuous, imperishable, immortal, incessant, cotinual, unceasing, unending, undying, ceaseless.
Ant. Limited, discontinuous, finite, brief, short, desultory, transitory, intermittent, periodic, recurrent.

Enemy
Syn. Rival, opponent, antagonist, foe, assailant, adversary.
Ant. Comrade, companion, associate, colleague, ally, friend confident.

Energy
Syn. Vigour, fervour, strength, power, might, zeal, potency.
Ant. Sleepiness, heaviness, weakness, lethargy, apathy.

Engage
Syn. Employ, occupy, engross, hire, promise, agree, stipulate, undertake, pledge.
Ant. Discharge, dismiss, remove, refuse, decline.

Enlarge
Syn. Expand, extend, grow, stretch out.
Ant. Reduce, decrease, diminish, lessen.

Enough
Syn. Sufficient, adequate, plenty, abundant, ample.
Ant. Insufficient, inadequate, scanty, deficient.

Enterprise
Syn. Boldness, daring, activity, energy.
Ant. Cowardice, pusillanimity, diffidence, timidity.

Enterprise
Syn. Venture, adventure, endeavour, effort, undertaking.
Ant. Cowardice, phenomenal, indolent, triffling.

Entice
Syn. Allure, charm, invite, draw, fascinate, captivate, endear.
Ant. Repulse, rebuff, reject, repel, defer, check.

Entire
Syn. Complete, whole, undivided, total, unbroken, full, thorough, solid, unmitigated.
Ant. Incomplete, partial, divided, imperfect.

Entrance
Syn. Entry, inlet, ingress, vestibule doorway, mouth, adit, portal, door.
Ant. Exit, outlet, egress.

Entrance
Syn. Arrival, entry, beginning, commencement, door, admission.
Ant. End, exit, dismisal, dipatch.

Erase
Syn. Cancel, abolish, destroy, wipe out, abrogate, rescind, invalidate, delete.
Ant. Confirm, establish, reinstate, insert, renew, engrave, ratify, restore, imprint.

Erect
Syn. Set up, construct, raise, build, elevate, institute.
Ant. Overthrow, destroy, raze, demolish, dismantle, break.

Erect
Syn. Vertical, firm, upright, still.
Ant. Horizontal, bent, stooping, slanting.

Error

Syn. Inaccuracy, mistake, fallacy, misapprehension, fault, hallucination, blunder.

Ant. Accuracy, correctness, truth, verify, exactitude.

Especial

Syn. Unusual, particular, extraordinary, distinctive, peculiar,
exceptional, unique, specific.

Ant. Unusual, general, ordinary, common, customary, habitual,
wanted.

Essential

Syn. Necessary, indispensable, requisite, vital, innate.

Ant. Unnecessary, superfluous, excessive, needless, useless,
inessential, redundant.

Establish

Syn. Found, fit, organise, institute, constitute, settle.

Ant. Demolish, break down, disorganise, overthrow, dismantle,
disband.

Establish

Syn. Confirm, ratify, prove, substantiate, demonstrate, verify.

Ant. Negative, confine, disapprove.

Evasion

Syn. Tergiversation, quibble, subterfuge, prevarication, excuse,
pretext.

Ant. Refutation, reply, rejoinder, response, defence, answer,.

Even

Syn. Equal, steady, uniform, regular, flat, constant, equable, smooth,
flush.

Ant. Unequal, unsteady, ununiform, irregular, wavering, fluctuating,
changeable, wavy.

Even

Syn. Fair, equitable, just, staighforward, impartial.

Ant. Unfair, inequitable, unjust, biased, partial, prejudiced.

Ever

Syn. Perpetually, always, continually, forever, eternally.

Ant. Never.

Evident

Syn. Clear, visible, obvious, patent, manifest, distinct.

Ant. Hidden, obscure, obstruse, secret, covert, latent, masked.

Exact

Syn. Truthful, unerring, correct, careful, precise, strict.

Ant. Untruthful, inexact, erring, incorrect, careless, negligent.

Examine

Syn. Scan, study, scrutnise, probe, explore, supervise, investigate, overhaul, inspect.

Ant. Disregard, overlook, ignore.

Example

Syn. Illustration, sample, quotation, model.

Ant. Vagueness, brevity, confusion, muddleheadedness, precept, theory.

Excel

Syn. Outdo, exceed, transcend, outvie, outweigh, beat, outstrip.

Ant. Dismay, decrease, eclipse.

Exchange

Syn. Substitute, truck, reciprocate, commute, stir, trade, interchange.

Ant. Indifferent, non-dealing, renounced.

Excite

Syn. Stimulate, provoke, awake, inflame, animate, kindle, arouse, irritate.

Ant. Compose, soothe, allay, hush, mollify, quell, appease, quieten, pacify, lull.

Exclusive

Syn. Excluding, omitting, excepting, debarring, snobbish, only, alone, aristocratic, special.

Ant. Including, embracing, inclusive, enclosing.

Excuse

Syn. Remit, pardon, overlook, condone, forgive, justify, absolve, acquit, free, exempt, apologise.

Ant. Accuse, charge, implicate, involve.

Exertion

Syn. Energy, strain, effort, stretch, pull, tug, spurt, bout, struggle, pains, trouble, endeavour, drill.

Ant. Rest, repose, peace, tranquillity, idleness, laziness.

Exhibition

Syn. Pageant, parade, display, spectacle, pomp, demonstration, reveal, exhibit, unfold, blazon, divulge, demonstrate, prove, evince.

Ant. Cover, hide, mask, conceal, veil, suppress, dissemble.

Existence

Syn. Truth, life, entity, positiveness, fact, reality, being, matter of fact, presence.

Ant. Inexistence, non-entity, nothingness, void, vacuum, oblivion, blank, nullity, negativeness, non-subsistence.

Expand

Syn. Increase, amplify, enlarge, spread, develop, distend, stretch.

Ant. Decrease, diminish, contract, curtail, reduce, condense, shorten, lessen.

Expansion

Syn. Amplification, spreading, distension, extension, stretching, increase.

Ant. Shrink, shirk, evaporate, cut-short.

Expectation

Syn. Hope, faith, belief, anticipation, foresight, prediction, expectancy, reckoning, lookout, prospect.

Ant. Dubiousness, discredit, unbelief, dubiety, jealousy, disbelief, irreligion.

Expert

Syn. Master, top sawyer, practised eye, top man, adept, virtuose, sharp, wizard, whip.

Ant. Inexperienced, apprentice, raw, unskilful, green horn, pupil.

Explain

Syn. Decipher, clear up, interpret, elucidate, teach, expand, unfold.

Ant. Obscure, conceal, disguise, obfuscate.

Extend

Syn. Expand, increase, amplify, augment, grow, stretch out, dilute.

Ant. Reduce, decrease, curtail, diminish, lessen, abate.

Extra

Syn. Unusual, extra-ordinary, special, extreme, supplemental, spare, additional, accessory, supplementary.

Ant. Limited, restricted, bounded, normal.

Extraordinary

Syn. Unusual, uncommon, remarkable, peculiar, wonderful, strange, noticeable, signal.

Ant. Usual, common, ordinary, normal, customary, habitual, commonplace, everyday.

Extravagant

Syn. Unreasonable, excessive, immoderate, inordinate, spendthrift, lavish, profuse, wasteful, prodigal.

Ant. Reasonable, judicious, moderate, temperate, economical, miserly, provident, thrifty, sparing.

Extreme

Syn. Excessive, immoderate, extravagant.

Ant. Temperate, moderate.

Extreme

Syn. Most, distant, outermost, terminal, farthest, final ultimate.

Ant. Primary, original, initial, first, introductory, primal.

Fast
Syn. Date, encounter, oppose, meet, confront, cover, level, coat, smooth, encrust.
Ant. Avoid, elude, eschew, shun.

Face
Syn. Physignomy, visage, surface, appearance, countenance, front, expression.
Ant. Back, invisible, concealment.

Facility
Syn. Easiness, smoothness, smooth, pilancy, snap, cinch, flexibility, capability, dexterity, skill, waver.
Ant. Difficulty, hardness, uphill, tough job, hard task, crossfire, Gordian knot, mess, maze, net, coil, puzzle.

Fact
Syn. Certainty, event, reality, phenomenon.
Ant. Falsehood, untruth, lying, forgery, fraud, distortion, fencing, shuffling, deceit.

Failure
Syn. Breakdown, collapse, omission, default, neglect, insolvency, bankruptcy, ruin, decay, decline, deficiency, neglect.
Ant. Attainment, achievement, victory, success, triumph.

Faithfulness
Syn. Loyalty, constancy, steadfastness, fidelity, devotion.
Ant. Disloyalty, inconstancy, untrustworthiness, unfaithfulness, infidelity, treachery.

False
Syn. Untrue, unreliable, fallacious, untruthful, fictitious, incorrect, bogus, misleading, deceptive, mendacious.
Ant. True, reliable veracious, truthful, authentic, correct.

False
Syn. Teacherous, faithless, perfidious, counterfeit, spurious, forged.
Ant. Devoted, loyal, faithful, reliable, trustworthy, trusty, real, original, genuine, authentic.

Fame
Syn. Repute, honour, glory, renown, credit, reputation.
Ant. Disrepute, honour, notoriety, oblivion.

Familiarity
Syn. Impudence, forwardness, fellowship, intimacy, knowledge.
Ant. Contempt, strangeness, disregard, unfamiliarity, hate.

Family
Syn. Children, forefathers, kindered, lineage, clan, tribe, descendants.
Ant. Loneliness, orphanage, individuality, unmarriendness, childlessness.

Famous
Syn. Renowned, famed, celebrated, reputable, distinguished, illustrious, eminent.
Ant. Fameless, notorious, unknown, obscure, anonymous.

Fanciful
Syn. Imaginary, unreal, imaginative, fantastic, capricious, whimsical.
Ant. Positive, real, existent, substantial, factual, veritable.

Far
Syn. Long way, distant, remote, protracted.
Ant. Adjacent, closeby, near, approaching, impending.

Farewell
Syn. Parting, leave-taking, goodbye, departure, Godspeed.
Ant. Welcome, home-coming, reception.

Farming
Syn. Cultivation, tilling, plantation, gardening, agriculture.
Ant. Plundering, desertation, destruction, spoiling.

Fast
Syn. Speedy, quick, swift, rapid, fleet, dissipated, reckless, thriftless, wild, extravagant.
Ant. Sluggish, slow, slack, tardy, dilatory; restrained, sedate, temperate, sober, abstemious.

Fast
Syn. Steady, stable, firm, unyielding, steadfast. constant.
Ant. Unsteady, unstable, loose, undependable.

Fatal
Syn. Lethal, pernicious, mortal, baneful, deadly, destructive.
Ant. Helpful, beneficial.

Fault
Syn. Spot, imperfection, defect, blemish, flaw, failing, stain.
Ant. Spotless, perfection, beauty, faultlessness, quality, excellence.

Fear
Syn. Awe, apprehension, consternation, trepidation, terror, dead, alarm.
Ant. Pluck, courage, fearlessness, bravery, valour, daring, boldness.

Feast
Syn. Banquet, holiday, festival, spread, repast, picnic.
Ant. Fast, starvation, hunger, famine, insufficiency, appetite.

Feeble
Syn. Weak, impotent. frail, languid, enervated, debiliated, infirm.
Ant. Strong, vigorous, muscular, athletic, stalwart, robust, sinewy.

Fiction
Syn. Falsehood, myth, fabrication, invention, story, tale, fable, romance.
Ant. Truth, reality, fact.

Fierce
Syn. Wild, savage, barbarous, violent, ferocious, ranging.
Ant. Gentle, subdued, tame, docile, domesticated.

Fight
Syn. War, battle, action, contest, conflict.
Ant. Peace, agreement, quiet, amity.

Filthy
Syn. Dirty, squalid, foul, impure, sullied.
Ant. Pure, clean, immaculate, spotless, unsullied, unsoiled.

Final

Syn. Ultimate, last, terminal, eventual, latest.

Ant. Primary, first, leading, preliminary, foremost.

Fit

Syn. Proper, decent, suitable, apt, becoming, decorous, seemly, right, fitting, meet, appropriate, adept, prepare, equip, furnish, provide.

Ant. Improper, indecent, unsuitable, unbecoming, indecorous, unseemly, unfit.

Fix

Syn. Connect, join, bind, attach, tie, fasten.

Ant. Disconnect, disjoin, unbind, divide, part, disunite separate, sever.

Fix

Syn. Secure, fasten, root, establish, plant, rivet, define, settle, determine, decide.

Ant. Eradicate, remove, uproot.

Flatter

Syn. Praise, compliment, wheedle, cajole, adulate, eulogise.

Ant. Insult, abuse, offend, affront.

Flexible

Syn. Plaint, lissom, pliable, yielding, lithe, complaint.

Ant. Unplaint, stiff. rigid, unyielding, inflexible, unbending, austere.

Flight

Syn. Retreat, exodus, stampede, rout, flying, mounting, volition, soaring.

Ant. Advent, return, arrival.

Fold

Syn. Enfold, furl, wrap, envelop.

Ant. Unfold, unfurl, open, unroll, display.

Follow

Syn. Observe, obey, heed, spring, arise, succeed, result, proceed, pursue, hunt, copy, chase, imitate.

Ant. Ignore, disobey, disregard.

Folly

Syn. Fatuity, foolishness, madness, imbecility, silliness, absurdity, stupidity.

Ant. Reason, discernment, sapience, wisdom, sagacity, prudence, sense.

Fond

Syn. Loving, doting, enamoured, attached, affection.

Ant. Adverse opposed, hostile, loath, averse.

Foolish

Syn. Senseless, irrational, unwise, injudicious, indiscreet, asinine, nonsensical, stupid, idiotic, unreasonable absurd.

Ant. Sensible, rational, wise, judicious, discreet, sane, sagacious, intelligent, sound.

Footstep

Syn. Vestige, mark, track, footprint.

Ant. Traceless, undiscovered, tracklessness.

Force

Syn. Emphasis, energy, might, strength, pressure, stress, vigour, power.

Ant. Persuasion, cajoling, coaxing.

Force

Syn. Coercion, compulsion, enforcement, violence, host, squadron, battalion, troop, army, legion.

Force

Syn. Enforce, coerce, compel, impel, constrain.

Ant. Coax, persuade, cajole, wheedle.

Foresight

Syn. Fore-knowledge, prudence, forethought, second sight, presentment, foreshadowing, futurity.

Ant. Narrow-mindness, bias, short sightedness, prejudice.

Forget

Syn. Neglect, overlook.

Ant. Recollect, recall, remember.

Forgive

Syn. Acquit, discharge, excuse, pardon.

Ant. Chastise, punish, penalise.

Formal

Syn. Methodical, regular, fixed, set, essential, stiff, ceremonious, pompous, correct, exact.

Ant. Unmethodical, irregular, loose, disorderly, unsettled, easy, unceremonious, unconventional, informal.

Fortunate

Syn. Favourable, auspicious, propitious, providential, lucky, successful, happy.

Ant. Unfavourable, inauspicious, unpropitious, unfortunate, unlucky.

Fortune

Syn. Riches, felicity, property, possession, wealth, affluence, opulence, future, hazard, doom, chance, destiny, luck, fate, lot.

Ant. Poverty, destitution, impecuniosity, privation, want, penury, indigence.

Forward

Syn. Premature, progressive, onward, advanced, presuming, bold, presumptuous, confident, early.

Ant. Overdue, primitive, archaic, late, unassuming, shy, unpretentious, retiring, modest.

Forward

Syn. Encourage, foster, speed up, accelerate, hurry, urge on, quicken, advance, hasten, expedite.

Ant. Discourage, delay, hinder, obstruct, oppose, restrain, retard, check.

Forward

Syn. Post, transmit, despatch, mail, send, ship.

Ant. Take, capture, to assume, swallow.

Fraud

Syn. Deceit, imposture, imposition, duplicity, stratagem, deception.

Ant. Honesty, probity, integrity.

Freedom

Syn. Independence, liberty, emancipation.

Ant. Slavery, thraldom, captivity, servitude, bondage.

Freedom

Syn. Looseness, licence, informality, laxness, familiarity, privilege, franchise, exemption.

Ant. Banc, bandit, outlaw, band, entanglement.

Frequent

Syn. Common, usual, familiar, customary, habitual, constant, repeated, many, persistent, recurrent, numerous.

Ant. Uncommon, unusual, rare, exceptional, choice, odd, infrequent, sparse.

Friend

Syn. Rival, opponent, antagonist, foe, assailant.

Ant. Comrade, companion, associate, colleague.

Fright

Syn. Apprehension, panic, terror, trepidation, consternation, fear, dismay, dread.

Ant. Tranquillity, calmness, coolness, equanimity, placidity, composure, peaceful.

Front

Syn. Anterior, obverse, face, frontage, van, forepart, breast, head.

Ant. Rear, posterior, back, wake, stern, tail, end.

Front

Syn. Confront, face, encounter, oppose.

Ant. Shrink, retreat, recoil, withdraw, cover.

Fundamental

Syn. Primary, essential, basic, constitutional, organic, entire, complete, underlying, indispensable.

Ant. Subsidiary, minor, petty, inferior, unimportant.

Funny

Syn. Comic, farcical, diverting, humorous, droll, amusing, grotesque, ludicrous, entertaining.

Ant. Serious, grave, sedate, sober, staid, solemn.

G

Gain
Syn. Lucre, winning, emolument, earnings, advantage, profit, benefit.
Ant. Forfeiture, loss, waste, deprivation.

Gain
Syn. Win, secure, arrive at, get, earn, benefit, reap, obtain, realise.
Ant. Lose, waste, mislay, forfeit, squander.

Gap
Syn. Cranny, cavity, crack, hollow, chasm, hole, chink, breach, crevice, interstice.
Ant. Pustule, pimple, swelling, elevation.

Gay
Syn. Cheerful, jovial, vivacious, jolly, sprightly, buoyant, joyous, blithe, festal.
Ant. Mournful, cheerless, unhappy, depressed, gloomy, sorrowful, sad, dismal.

Gay
Syn. Smart, bright, gaudy, brilliant, flaunting.
Ant. Dull, gloomy, dismal, doleful, lugubrious, sombre, funeral.

General
Syn. Common, usual, ordinary, indefinite, inaccurate, ill-defined, vague, loose, total, whole.
Ant. Uncommon, unusual, exceptional, specific, rare, definite, accurate, well-defined, exacting.

Generous
Syn. Magnanimous, liberal, bountiful, munificent, noble.
Ant. Greedy, mean, parsimonious, miserly, illiberal, stingy.

Genius
Syn. Talent, bent, gift, ability, skill.
Ant. Buffoon, jester, joker, chimp, bonehead, dunce, blockhead, goose, ninny, halfwit, nitwit, idiot.

Gentleness
Syn. Moderation, kindness, lenience, mildness.
Ant. Violence, harshness; wickedness, roughness.

Gifted
Syn. Intelligent, able, apt, skillful, sagacious, talented.
Ant. Foolish, stupid, asinine, idiotic, stolid.

Give
Syn. Impart, confer, furnish, accord, contribute, donate, supply.
Ant. Keep, reserve, suppress, detain, withhold, retain.

Glad
Syn. Cheerful, delightful, cheering, joyful, pleasing, delight, pleased, happy, merry, elated, gratified.
Ant. Cheerless, sorrowful, melancholy, mournful, dismal, sad, sorrow, grieved, dejected, depressed.

Gloomy
Syn. Shadow, dark, dim, dusky, lurid, dismal, depressing, lowering, dispiriting, cheerless.
Ant. Light, bright, illuminated, exhilarating, cheering, enlivening.

Gloomy
Syn. Sad, dejected, glum, depressed, saddening, dispirited, despondent, melancholy.
Ant. Happy, jocund, cheerful, merry, gay, lively, jolly.

Glory
Syn. Brightness, brilliance, splendour, pomp, honour, renown, celebrity, exaltation, nobleness, fame.
Ant. Dullness, dimness, tarnish, cloudiness, baseness, meanness, insignificance, vileness.

God
Syn. Divinity, creator, Lord, image, idol, Almighty, deity.
Ant. Devil, Satan, Lucifer, Demon.

Good

Syn. Beneficial, useful, serviceable, profitable, skilful, able, expert, dexterous, competent, just, righteous, excellent, upright, worthy, true.

Ant. Harmful, detrimental, noxious, baneful, unskilful, useless, clumsy, bungling, unapt, maladroit, wicked, corrupt, dishonest, immoral, bad, depraved.

Good

Syn. Advantage, benefit, gain, welfare, prosperity, morality, righteous-ness, virtue, excellence.

Ant. Injury, harm, disadvantage, detriment, prejudice, corruption, wickedness, depravity, malignity.

Gorgeous

Syn. Sumptuous, magnificent, splendid, grand.

Ant. Colourless, simple, unadorned, sombre.

Govern

Syn. Rule, manage, control, direct, command, supervise.

Ant. Misrule, mismanage, misgovern.

Government

Syn. Dominion, administration, rule, control, autonomy, regulation.

Ant. Mismanagement, maladministration, misrule, disorder, anarchy.

Graceful

Syn. Lovely, elegant, becoming, comely.

Ant. Uncouth, awkward, lumbering, ungraceful, ungainly.

Gradual

Syn. Slow, regular, continuous, progressive.

Ant. Rapid, momentary, unanticipated, unpremeditated, unforeseen, unacted.

Grand

Syn. Noble, majestic, lordly, stately, resplendent, august, superb, exalted, princely, illustrious.

Ant. Inferior, colourless, poor, dingy, mediocre, lowly.

Grant

Syn. Concession, salary, donation, gift, present, wages, benefaction, largeness, allowance.

Ant. Fine, tax excise, surcharge, penalty.

Grant
Syn. Impart, allot, give, yield, admit, concede, allow.
Ant. Retain, reserve, keep, withhold.

Gratitude
Syn. Thankfulness, worship, gratefulness, indebtedness, thanks-offering.
Ant. Thanklessness, cruelty, heartlessness, ingratitude, in-humanity.

Grave
Syn. Solemn, sedate, sober, sombre, staid.
Ant. Jacose, gay, cheerful, joyous, jovial, hilarious, lively, merry, jolly.

Greatness
Syn. Fullness, eminence, magnitude, strength, power, multitude, notability, fame, repute.
Ant. Littleness, pettiness, smallness, insignificance.

Greedy
Syn. Rapacious, gluttonous, eager, grasping, voracious.
Ant. Moderate, generous, abstemious, magnanimous, unselfish.

Greeting
Syn. Hail, welcome, salutation.
Ant. Valediction, farewell, adieu, good-bye.

Grief
Syn. Plain, sorrow, trouble, affliction, bereavement, distress.
Ant. Glee, joy, contentment, satisfaction, happiness, pleasure.

Grim
Syn. Horrible, awful, ferocious, fierce, grisly, appaling, terrible, cruel, savage.
Ant. Gentle, benevolent, gracious, friendly, humane, benign.

Grip
Syn. Hold, clutch, grasp, seize.
Ant. Free, unhand, liberate, unloose, release.

Groundless
Syn. False, baseless, unauthorised, gratuitous, fanciful.
Ant. Actual, material, well-founded, substantial, positive, real, solid.

Group

Syn. Collection, assemblage, crowd, clump, bunch, cluster, order, class.

Ant. Individual, single, solitary.

Guess

Syn. Fancy, conjecture, divine, suppose, surmise, reckon, think, imagine.

Ant. Substantiate, prove, deduce, conclude, infer, establish, justify, evince.

Guest

Syn. Visitor, caller, stranger, friend.

Ant. Permanent, family man, host, boarder.

Guilt

Syn. Sinfulness, misconduct, misdoing, guiltiness, chargeability, failing, offence, deadly sin, outrage.

Ant. Sinlessness, innocence, holiness, virtue, goodness.

Habit
Syn. Rule, usage, habitude, fashion, nature, use.
Ant. Irregularity, fashionlessness, disuse.

Hair
Syn. Tresses, filament, hirsuteness, mops, lock, thatch, nap, glory.
Ant. Hairlessness, baldness, smoothness.

Hand
Syn. Employee, helper, extremity, fist, handwriting, workman, labourer.
Ant. Employer, director, receiving.

Handle
Syn. Manage, wield, direct, use, manipulate, discuss, deal, treat.
Ant. Bungle, mess up, botch, mishandle, throw.

Handy
Syn. Skilled, skilful, expert, adroit, proficient, dexterous, ready, close, near, convenient.
Ant. Unskilled, unskilful, bungling, blundering, clumsy, unhandy.

Handsome
Syn. Beautiful, comely, lovely, charming, elegant, fair, pleasing.
Ant. Ugly, loathsome, unsightly, unlovely, uncomely, hideous, ungainly.

Hang
Syn. Put up, dangle, drape, execute, fasten, drop, trail.
Ant. Go, stagnate, move, act, lower, stand.

Happen
Syn. Change, occur, befall, betide.
Ant. Mishap, misfortune, dumps.

Happy
Syn. Lucky, joyous, gay, glad, ecstatic, contented, fortunate.
Ant. Unlucky, gloomy, sad, sorry, unhappy, dejected, sullen.

Harm
Syn. Evil, ill, injury, hurt, mishap, mischief, damage, wickedness.
Ant. Good, advantage, prosperity, benefit, gain, welfare, weal.

Harm
Syn. Moles, injure, damage, desecrate, abuse, hurt, maltreat.
Ant. Benefit, serve, avail, befriend, help, enrich.

Harsh
Syn. Jarring, raucous, unmusical, discordant, strident.
Ant. Musical, concordant, tuneful, melodious, dull.

Hate
Syn. Despise, detest, loathe, abhor, abominate.
Ant. Esteem, love, adore, like.

Hatred
Syn. Dislike, abhorrence, animosity, disgust, repugnance, antipathy, abomination, loathing, aversion, detestation.
Ant. Liking, affection, fondness, adoration, love, attachment.

Have
Syn. Be in possession, be possessed of, hold, occupy, own, possess.
Ant. Need, lack, want, require.

Hazard
Syn. Accident, chance, danger, jeopardy, risk, venture, peril, fortuity, contingency.
Ant. Assurance, certainty, necessity, plan, protection, safeguard, security, surety.

Healthy
Syn. Hale, hygienic, sanitary, vigorous, well, wholesome, strong, sound, salutary, salubrious, hearty, healthful.
Ant. Wasted, unsound, failing exhausted, unhealthy, ill, sick, worn, frail, delicate, diseased.

Help
Syn. Support, co-operate, relief, contribute, assist.
Ant. Check, hindrance, hinder, deter, retard.

67

Hesitate

Syn. Waver, dubitate, tarry, totter, pause, demur.

Ant. Determine, settle, end, decide, resolve.

Hide

Syn. Bury, inter, screen, veil, secret, entomb, overwhelm, disguise, dissemble.

Ant. Unveil, betray, avow, exhume, expose, lay bare, raise, publish, unmask, uncover, fell, show, disinter, divulge, exhibit, admit.

High

Syn. Elevated, exalted, noble, steep, towering, uplifted, tall, eminent.

Ant. Base, stunted, short, deep, degraded, depressed, low, proud, inferior.

Hire

Syn. Engage, lease, commission, charter, secure, employ.

Ant. Purchase, discharge, buy, fire, retire.

History

Syn. Account, recital, story, register, record, biography, narrative, memorial, autobiography, archives, annals, memoir.

Ant. Allegory, fabrication, figment, myth, story, novel, invention, legend, falsehood, apologue, fable.

Hole

Syn. Aperture, crack, crater, defile, den, dent, fissure, gap, forge, hold, hollow, valley, vale, tube, slit, mine, depression, cell, chasm, cleft, bore.

Ant. Convexity, elevation, rising, rampart, prominence, hillock, hill, lamp, mound, eminence, height, mountain.

Holy

Syn. Religious, godly, saintly, sacred, devout, divine.

Ant. Irreligious, ungodly, godless, irreverent, sacrilegious, profane.

Home

Syn. Abode, dwelling, habitation, house, residence, hearth, fireside, domicile.

An. Desert, ethercal, wilderness, a waste.

Honest

Syn. Honourable, sincere, trustworthy, virtuous, genuine, upright, straightforward.

Ant. Dishonest, deceitful, untrustworthy, dissembling.

Honour
Syn. Probity, integrity, repute, title, glory, fame, respect, distinction, worship.

Ant. Dishonour, infamy, unpopularity, disrepute, disrespect, notoriety.

Hope
Syn. Trust, confidence, anticipation, expectancy, anticipate, await.

Ant. Desperation, despair, hopelessness, despondency.

Horrible
Syn. Frightful, appalling, dire, ghastly, ugly, fearful, awful, terrific, dreadful, hideous, repulsive.

Ant. Agreeable, pleasant, delightful, pleasurable, charming, pleasing.

Hospitality
Syn. Welcome, cordiality, entertainment, sociability.

Ant. Coldness, cold shoulder, icy, welcome.

Humble
Syn. Complaint, lowly soft, unostentatious, deferential, meek, mild, unassuming, yielding, gentle, modest.

Ant. Arrogant, assuming, bold, choleric, proud, vengeful, stubborn, wrathful, wilful, haughty, obstinate, presumptuous.

Humour
Syn. Wit, fun, drollery, pleasantry, amusement, jocularity.

Ant. Solemnity, gravity, sobriety, seriousness.

Hunt
Syn. Mood, temper, caprice, fancy, whim, disposition.

Ant. Leisure, unpreparedhen, rigid, severe.

Hurt
Syn. Injure, damage, harm, wound, impair, mar, spoil, bruise, pain, grieve, offend.

Ant. Enrich, benefit, help, profit, serve.

Hypocrisy
Syn. Deceit, pretence, falsify, deception, insincerity, cant.

Ant. Honesty, uprightness, straight forwardness.

Idea
Syn. Notion, conception, supposition, thought, opinion imagination, doctrine, impression.

Ant. Truth, actuality, fact, reality, verity.

Ideal
Syn. Archetype, model, prototype, example, standard, original, pattern.

Ant. Accomplishment, act, realisation, practice, fact, attainment, executions, incarnation, achievement.

Identical
Syn. Alike, synonymous, same, tantamount, interchangeable, selfsame, equivalent.

Ant. Different, opposite, contrast, autonymous.

Idle
Syn. Inert, unoccupied, lazy, inactive, slothful, sluggish, unemployed.

Ant. Active, busy, diligent, industrious, assiduous.

Ignorance
Syn. Illiteracy, unexplored, ground, simpleness, simplicity, blindness, darkness, soil.

Ant. Acquaintance, wisdom, light, intelligence.

Image
Syn. Resemblance, statue, picture, likeness, representation, effigy.

Ant. Unidentical, contrast, contradictory.

Imitate
Syn. Budesque, echo, follow, copy, impersonate, mock, mimic, counterfeit, forge, parody.

Ant. Alter, convert, modify, vary.

Immediately
Syn. At once, now right off, without delay, this instant, right away, intantly, instant.
Ant. After a while, in future, by and by, hereafter.

Imminent
Syn. Impending, threatening.
Ant. Chimerical, unlikely, doubtful, contingent, problematical, improbable.

Impartial
Syn. lkunprejudiced, neutral, just, unbiased, fair equitable.
Ant. Partial, unfair, unjust, biased, prejudiced.

Impertinence
Syn. Assurance, boldnes, forwardness, sauciness, rudeness, pertness, insolence, incivility, impudence, presumption.
Antl. Bashfulness, coyness, submisiveness, modesty, meekness, lowlines, diffidence.

Importance
Syn. Important, significance, moment, mark, primacy, value worth, greatness, superiority, distinction, concern, interest.
Ant. Unimportance, insignificance, pettines, purpoeleseness, meanness.

Important
Syn. Consequential, great, prominent, weighty, serious, relevant, materil, essential, grave, momentous, powerful, prominent, critical.
Ant. Feeble, flimsy,, worthless, ueless, lunnecesary, petty, nonessential, slight, secondary, incosiderable, frivolour, idle.

impossible
Syn. Absurd, unreasonable, out of reach, out of question, impracticable, incredible, hopeless, improbable.
Ant. Possible, probable, practical.

Improve
Syn. Amend, correct, reform, rectify, ameliorate, better, increase.
Ant. Spoil, deteriorate, corrupt, mar, damage, deprecate, impair.

Inability
Syn. Disability, impotence, incapability.
Ant. Ability, capability, power.

Incapable
Syn. Incompetent, inefficient, unqualified, inadequate, unable, unfit.
Ant. Gifted, capable, qualified, accomplished, competent, efficient.

Increase
Syn. Enlargement, extension, dilation, rise, profit, advance, spread, flood, gain, increment, tide.
Ant. Reduce, decline, subside, diminish.

Indecent
Syn. Indelicate, lewd, indecorous, unchaste, improper, shameless, filthy, foul.
Ant. Decent, seemly, pure, moral, proper, virtuous, chaste, decorous.

Inference
Syn. Conclusion, consequence, deduction, induction, judgment.
Ant. Unsettlement, disarrange, not in order, confused, mixed.

Inferior
Syn. Imperfect, deficient.
Ant. Perfect, superlative.

Inferior
Syn. Secondary, lower, lesser, junior, minor, subordinate.
Ant. Senior, superior, chief, head, principal.

Infinite
Syn. Interminable, unmeasured, unlimited, limitless, unbounded, unfathomable, eternal, countless.
Ant. Bounded, brief, circumscribed, narrow, restricted, transistory, small, short, shallow, transient.

Influence
Syn. Actuate, draw, excite, incline, lead, prompt, urge, move, induce, stir, drive, incite, compel.
Ant. Retard, dissuade, hinder, deter, prevent, inhibit, restrain.

Inform
Syn. Tell, make known, instruct, apprise, enlighten, notify, acquaint.
Ant. Confuse, preplex, puzzle, mystify, bewilder.

Inherent
Syn. Congenital, inhering, ingrained, infixed, internal, innate, subjective, native, inwrought, natural, inborn.

Ant. Unconnected, supplemental, superficial, fortuitous, external, casual, subsidiary, accidental.

Injure
Syn. Aggrieve, wrong, disfigure, mar, damage, harm, spoil, sully, deteriorate.

Ant. Benefit, aid, improve, enrich, help.

Injury
Syn. Evil, hurt, loss, mischief, damage.

Ant. Atonement, compensation, amend, recompense, reparation, redress.

Injustice
Syn. Grievance, injury, unfairness, wrong, tort, unrighteousness.

Ant. Equity, fairness, fair play, faithfulness, honesty, rectitude, justice, lawfulness, impartiality, integrity.

Innocent
Syn. Blameless, guileless, innoxious, right, pure, stainless, sinless, upright, harmless, immaculate, innocuous, righteous.

Ant. Wicked, guilty, culpable, blameable, criminal.

Inquiry
Syn. Question, request, search, quest, test, examination, study, hearing, trial, prove, sifting.

Ant. Answer, reply, information, response.

Insanity
Syn. Aberration, dementia, lunacy, madness, mania, frenzy, derangement, delirium, craziness.

Ant. Sanity, rationality, good sense, clearness, lucidity.

Insist
Syn. Urge, persist, contend, demand, maintain, persevere.

Ant. Relinquish, forgo, waive, renounce, abandon.

Inspect
Syn. Scan, study, scrutinise, inspect, explore.

Ant. Disregard, over look, ignore.

Instruct
Syn. Teach, school, edify, educate, indoctrinate, enlighten, inform.
Ant. Fool, beguile, dupe, gull, deceive, delude, mislead.

Insufficient
Syn. Incapable, lacking, scanty, deficient, incompetent, inadequate.
Ant. Sufficient, ample, plenty, profuse, adequate, abundant.

Intelligent
Syn. Well-informed, discerning, shrewd, bright, clever, enlightened, instructed.
Ant. Dull, stolid, stupid, doltish, unintelligent, foolish.

Intensify
Syn. Aggravate, heighten, magnify, made worse, increase, enhance.
Ant. Lessen, diminish, attenuate, reduce, alleviate, assuage.

Intolerance
Syn. Bias, narrowness, dogmatism, prejudice.
Ant. Tolerance, forbearance, toleration, politeness.

Invent
Syn. Design contrive, create, discover, devise, find out, fabricate, originate.
Ant. Copy, imitate, duplicate.

Irregular
Syn. Wild, wandering, unsettled, uneven, immoderate, disorderly, fitful, exceptional, abnormal, confused, crooked, devious, erratic.
Ant. Usual, steady, systematic, uniform, formal, fixed, constant, natural, regular, stated, unvarying, periodical, universal.

Irritate
Syn. Exasperate, annoy, tease, offend, incense, vex, chafe, enrage, provoke, excite, anger, inflame, harsh.
Ant. Calm, reconcile, appease, assuage, propitiate, placate, soothe, allay, mollify.

J

Jealous
Syn. Covetous, envious, suspicious
Ant. Indifferent, liberal, genital.

Jesting
Syn. Joking, playing the fool, pun, gag, wit, aping, humour, clowning, jocularity.
Ant. Seriousness, tragedy, gravity, businessmanship.

Journey
Syn. Cruise, expedition, tour, passage, travel, transit, trip, voyage.
Ant. Stability, established, settled.

Judge
Syn. Jurist, justice court, justice, of peace, umpire, arbiter.
Ant. Critic, self-server, commander, dictator.

Jump
Syn. Bounce, vault, bound, spring, cape, skip, leap.
Ant. Sink, fall, drop.

Justice
Syn. Equity, virtue, legality, truth, justness, law, honour, integrity, fair, play, faithfulness.
Ant. Dishonesty, wrong, untruth, favourtism, inequity, unreasonableness, unfairness, partiality, injustice.

Keen
Syn. Nippy, enthusiastic, quick, shrewd, piercing, stinging, eager, edged, razorlike, cutting sharp.

Ant. Bluntness, laziness, follishness, dull, indifference, slow, stupid.

Keep
Syn. Carry, defend, maintain, protect, refrain support, sustain, retain, withhold, hold, guard, fulfil, detail, celebrate, conduct.

Ant. Discard, throw away, cast away, reject, neglect, ignore, disregard, overlook, cease, finish, destroy.

Kill
Syn. Assassinate, dispatch, massacre, murder, slaughter, put to death, butcher, execute.

Ant. Create, produce, fashion, cause, origniate.

Kind
Syn. Compassionate, benign, affable, generous, lenient, sympathetic, charitable, merciful, tender, philanthropic, complaisant, forbearing.

Ant. Cruel, callous, unfeeling, unkind, hard-hearted, insensible, hard, harsh.

Kind
Syn. Species, genus, style, sort, make, brand, manner, nature, type, race, caste, family, category.

Ant. Common, usual, customary.

Knowledge
Syn. Acquaintance, perception, science, wisdom, intuition, comprehension, cognition, information, lore, light, intelligence.

Ant. Ignorance, unfamiliarity, misunderstanding, misapprehension, inexperience, illiteracy.

Labour
Syn. Work, toil, exertion, drudgery, industry.
Ant. Repose, rest, relaxation, stillness.

Lack
Syn. Need, shortage, deficiency, want.
Ant. Sufficiency, prosperity, wealth, riches.

Language
Syn. Barbarism, expression, dialect, diction, mother tongue, vocabulary, vernacular, tongue, speech, patois.
Ant. Dumbness, action, unverbal, pure, posture.

Laughable
Syn. Comic, humorous, amusing, grotesque, ludicrous.
Ant. Serious, grave, sedate, sober.

Law
Syn. Canon, decree, formula, edict, economy, legislation, precept, order, mandate, polity, jurisprudence, rule, statute.
Ant. Anarchy, chaos, disorder, confusion.

Lazy
Syn. Idle, sluggish, indolent, unemployed, slow, slothful.
Ant. Active, smart, agile, up and doing.

Leader
Syn. Guide, guru, teacher, director, conductor, principal, politician.
Ant. Follower, trainee, apprentice, pupil, henchman.

Learn
Syn. Acquire, memorise, discover, detect, find out, trace.
Ant. Forget, unlearn, miss, misunderstand, ignore.

Liberty
Syn. Emancipation, freedom, independence, licence, permission.
Ant. Captivity, compulsion, constraint, imprisonment, slavery, serfdom, servitude, oppression, obligation, thraldom.

Lift
Syn. Exalt, erect, raise, elevate, hoist.
Ant. Drop, lower, sink, let fall.

Light
Syn. Beam, blaze, flash, flame, flare, glow, incandescence, shine, twinkle, gleaming, glistening, glitter, shimmer, sparkle.
Ant. Blackness, dark, shadow, shade, gloom, dusk, obscurity, gloominess.

Likely
Syn. Apt, reasonable, presumable, liable, credible, possible, conceivable, conjectural.
Ant. Doubtful, improbable, questionable, unlikely, dubious, unreasonable.

Listen
Syn. Hear, attend, mind, heed, hearken.
Ant. Ignore, overlook, disregard.

Live
Syn. Foolish, unintelligent, stupid.
Ant. Wise, intelligent, clever, talented.

Load
Syn. Burden, clog, freight, landing, pack, weight, incubus, cargo.
Ant. Unload, unpack, remove, detach.

Look
Syn. Behold, inspect, see, watch, view stare, gaze, descry, discern, observe, regard, survey.
Ant. Ignore, reject, veil, bypass.

Loss
Syn. Predition, forfeiture, lapse, destruction, leakage, riddance. bereave, privation.
Ant. Gain, profit, construction, acquisition, prosperity.

Love
Syn. Affection, fondness, charity, liking, regard, friendship, tenderness, attraction.
Ant. Hate, dislike, disgust.

Luck
Syn. Fortune, chance, prosperity, good stroke.
Ant. Bad luck, misfortune, bad stroke, unfavourable.

Lucky
Syn. Fortunate, prosperous, propitious, auspicious, favourable.
Ant. Unlucky, luckless, inauspicious, ill-fate, unfortunate.

Luxury
Syn. Self-indulgence, extravagance, sumptuousness, dainty.
Ant. Simplicity, commonness, ordinariness, plainness.

Majority
Syn. Adulthood, excess, superiority, preponderance.
Ant. Minority, smallness, inferiority.

Make
Syn. Construct, fashion, originate, produce, perform, reach, shape, frame, gait, do, create, establish, execute, fabricate, frame, compose, compel, cause.
Ant. Annihilate, mar, destroy, demolish, devastate, ravage, extirpate.

Manner
Syn. Style, mode, custom, method, system, way, fashion, conduct, behaviour.
Ant. Mannerlessness, discourtesy, unsocialness, unsystematic, unmethodical.

Marine
Syn. Nautical, naval, maritime, oceanic.
Ant. Land, earth, ground.

Marriage
Syn. Matrimony, wedlock, bed and board, wedded, engagement, married, state, cohabitation.
Ant. Bachelorhood, celibacy, divorce, maidenhood, widowhood, virginity.

Material
Syn. Raw material, stuff, brick and mortar, metal, stone, crockery, personal, property, staple, stock, substance.
Ant. Spirit, non-materials, invisibles, energy, sound, magnetism, light, heat, electricity.

Mean

Syn. Medium, golden mean, middle, course, middle of the road, fence-sitting, moderation, mediocrity.

Ant. Extreme, leftism, radicalism, extremity.

Melody

Syn. Unison, tune, symphony, music, harmony, air.

Ant. Discord, recitative, noise, distortion.

Memory

Syn. Mind, retrospection, reminiscence, remembrance, retrospect, recollection.

Ant. Frogetfulness, oblivion, oversight, unconsciousness.

Mention

Syn. Impart, tell, reveal, report, state, cite, name, disclose, communicate.

Ant. Omit, suppress, conceal, exclude.

Mercy

Syn. Benevolence, favour, pardon, clemency, compassion, gentleness, leniency, pity, mildness, grace, kindness.

Ant. Cruelty, hardness, harshness, vigour, severity, sternness, penalty, punishment.

Messenger

Syn. Precursor, envoy, forerunner, emissary, herald, harbinger, carrier, courier.

Ant. personally, by-self, self-activity.

Middle

Syn. Midst, hub, core, kernel, axis, narrow, pith, term, medium, mean, equator, middle, distance, focus, focal point.

Ant. Exterior, end, terminus, extreme.

Mild

Syn. Bland, soft, gentle, kind, docile, tender, meek, placid.

Ant. Wild, ferocious, blood-thirsty, fierce, brutish, savage.

Mind

Syn. Wit, thought, sense, reason, intellect, disposition, brain, intelligence, understanding, spirit.

Ant. Body, matter, brown, brute, force, material, substance.

Minute
Syn. Circumstantial, fine, tiny, small, slender, little, particular, exact, critical, detailed.

Ant. Abundant, coarse, huge, long, vast, wide, immense, great extensive, bulky, broad.

Miscellaneous
Syn. Assorted, mingled, motley, unlike, various, variant, mixed, dissimilar, discordant, confused, promiscuous.

Ant. Homogeneous, identical, like, pure, uniform, same, similar.

Mischief
Syn. Injury, hurt, damage, ill, harm.

Ant. Benefit, good, gain, welfare, advantage, profit.

Misery
Syn. Wretchedness, pain, anguish, privation, distress, discomfort, agony.

Ant. Prosperity, joy, pleasure, satisfaction, happiness.

Misfortune
Syn. Adversity, disaster, ill-luck, sorrow, ruin, trail, trouble, mishap, reverse, hardship, failure, ill, harm, mischance.

Ant. Blessing, triumph, boon, success, comfort, relief, consolation, pleasure, good, fortune, joy, goodluck, happiness.

Mislead
Syn. Misguide, deceive, delude, misdirect, beguile.

Ant. Pilot, guide, direct, steer, lead.

Mistake
Syn. Misapprehend, misunderstand, err, misinterpret, misconstrue, slip, misapprehension, defusion, blunder, error misconception, oversight.

Ant. Realise, understand, conceive, apprehend, perceive.

Mix
Syn. Compound, variety, confound, confuse, unite, co-mingle, miscellany, medley.

Ant. Disintegrate, separate, divide, detach, sort, segregate.

Mob
Syn. Riff-raff, common herd, populace, hoi, polloi, rabble.
Ant. Individual person, single, crusader.

Modern
Syn. New, recent, present, current, novel, new-fangled, up-to date, fresh.
Ant. Old, primitive, antiquated, ancient, archaic, obsolete.

Modesty
Syn. Backwardness, diffidence, reserve, timidity, coldness, shyness, unobtrusiveness, coyness.
Ant. Sociability, frankness, forwardness, impudence, indiscretion freedom, boldness, assurance, assumption, sauciness.

Moment
Syn. Trice, jiffy, second, instant, twinkling.
Ant. Epoch, generation, century, period, age.

Moral
Syn. Honourable, upright, just, ethical, strict, right, virtuous.
Ant. Immoral, dishonourable, vicious, unprincipled, unrighteous.

Motion
Syn. Act. action, change, move, passage, transit, transition, process, movement.
Ant. Immobility, rest, stillness, response, quite, quiescence.

Mourn
Syn. Bemoan, bewail, sorrow, lament, regret, grieve, deplore.
Ant. Bejoyful, joy, rejoice, triumph, made merry, exult.

Murder
Syn. Killing, assassination, end to life.
Ant. Revive, remedy, cure, bring to life.

Music
Syn. Symphony, rhythm, minstrelsy, melody, tune.
Ant. Discord, atonality, disharmony.

Mystery
Syn. Secret, hidden-precipe, enigma, concealed, wisdom.
Ant. Open hook, news, known, public, report.

Name
Syn. Agnomen, style, title, surname, denomination, appellation, epithet.
Ant. Untitled, common, non-authority, un-known.

Narrow
Syn. Straightened, cramped, pinched, confined, limited circumscribed, contracted, close, sparse, illiberal, intolerant, biased.
Ant. Wide, broad, vast, large, extensive, spacious, unlimited, unprejudiced, unbiassed, natural, disinterested, impartial.

Nation
Syn. Realm, state, land, country, community, race, commonwealth.
Ant. non-governed, un-devided, un-social, un-civilised.

Native
Syn. Aboriginal, innate, original, natural, indigenous.
Ant. Foreign, extraneous, alient, acquired, supplemented, extrinsic, adventitious.

Nearness
Syn. Propinquity, vicinity, proximity, neighbourhood, contiguity.
Ant. Distance, remoteness, separation.

Neat
Syn. Clean, spruce, trim, tidy, prim, natty, cleanly, orderly, dapper, nice.
Ant. Dirty, disorderly, uncared for, unkempt, untidy, slovenly, soiled, rough, rude.

Necessary
Syn. Essential, needful, required, requisite, undeniable, unavoidable, inevitable.
Ant. Casual, worthless, needless, non-essential, optional, unnecessary, useless.

Necessity
Syn. Compulsion, indispensability, want, urgency, need, requirement, unavoidableness, essential.
Ant. Choice, freedom, option, possibility, uncertainty, doubt, doubtfulness.

Neglect
Syn. Carelessness, neglectfulness, negligence, omission, oversight, slight, scorn, slackness, inadvertence, heedlessness, default failure, disregard, disrespect.
Ant. Care, attention, observation, adventure, heed.

Neighbour
Syn. Adjacent, dweller, next-door, lodger, next man, member of a community, brother, fellow-traveller.
Ant. Enmity, rivalry, religious, animosity, trickery.

Nervous
Syn. Hesitant, shaky, timid, timorous, afraid, agitated.
Ant. Courageous, bold, manly, undaunted, doughty, valiant, brave.

New
Syn. Unused, fresh, novel, recent, modern.
Ant. Old, ancient, aged, obsolete, antique, antiquated.

Nimble
Syn. Active, agile, prompt, flexible, quick, speedy, spry, swift.
Ant. Clumsy, unready, sluggish, inert, inactive, dull, dilatory.

Noble
Syn. Dignified, lofty, eminent, honourable, magnificent, great, illustrious, elevated, peer, lord, aristocrat, grandee.
Ant. Ignoble, mean, humble, common.

Noise
Syn. Hubbub, row, din, clamour, racket, outcry, tumult.
Ant. Peace, stillness, quietude, silence, repose, motionless.

Normal
Syn. Regular, typical, standard, wonted, natural, usual, ordinary.
Ant. Unusual, abnormal, exceptional, strange, uncommon, singular.

Non-existence
Syn. Inexistence, nullity, nihility, oblivion, blank, negativeness, nonentity.
Ant. Truth, life, entity, positiveness, fact, being.

Nonsense
Syn. Absurdity, folly, silliness, trash, good-for-nothingness, senselessness, simplicity, rusticity.
Ant. Sense, significance, importance, wisdom, meaning.

Nothing
Syn. Cipher, zero, blank, naught, nonentity, nothingness, trifle, unimportance.
Ant. Universality, omnipotence, everythingness.

Notion
Syn. Conception, impression, imagination, opinion, doctrine, belief, supposition, thought.
Ant. Truth, reality, fact, verity, actuality.

Notorious
Syn. Infamous, disreputable.
Ant. Reputable, famous, noted.

Numerous
Syn. Various, several, manifold, sundry, diverse.
Ant. Few, scarce, scanty, rare.

Oath
Syn. Epithet, curse, imprecation.
Ant. Non-realisation, nonfulfilment.

Obedient
Syn. Submissive, subservient, dutiful, tractable, yielding.
Ant. Mutinous, stubborn, intractable, disobedient, refratory.

Object
Syn. Contravene, take exception, oppose, hesitate, scruple, gainsay, disapprove.
Ant. Accept, concur, consent, approve, applaud, admit, comply, assent.

Obligatory
Syn. Necessary, unavoidable, needful, imperative, compulsory.
Ant. Desired, willing, voluntary, self-chosen.

Obscure
Syn. Dark, doubtful, dim, dense, hidden, dusky, muddy, turbid, involved, unintelligible, deep, darksome, cloudy.
Ant. Apparent, intelligible, lucid, plain, straightforward, transparent, unadorned, pellucid, obvious, evident, distinct.

Obsolete
Syn. Past, antiquated, discorded, outworn, extinct, dead.
Ant. Fresh, recent, modern, unused.

Obstacle
Syn. Difficulty, obstruction, snag, hurdle, hindrance, barrier, opposition, hardship.
Ant. Acid, encouragement, help, co-operation, facility.

Obstruct
Syn. Bar, check, thwart, retard, block, prevent, barricade, choke.
Ant. Forward, help further, assist, advance, promote, encourage.

Obvious
Syn. Clear, evident, visible, distinct, palpable, patent, discernible, perceptible.
Ant. Hidden, masked, veiled, covert, secret, obscure, concealed, latent.

Offence
Syn. Insult, disgrace, attack, discourtesy, fault, crime, sin.
Ant. Defence, meekness, politeness, modesty, grace, courtesy.

Offer
Syn. Adduce, hold out, extend, proffer, present, tender, volunteer, bid, attempt.
Ant. Alienate, withdraw, retract, retain, divert, withhold.

Old
Syn. Ancient, antiquated, matured, original, elderly, old-fashioned, aged, primitive, antique.
Ant. Fresh, unused, recent, modern.

Omen
Syn. Portent, augury, sign, premonition, presage, foreboding.
Ant. Historical, of late, universal.

Omit
Syn. Overlook, miss, skip, neglect, pass over, fail, exclude.
Ant. Include, embody, comprise, embrace.

Onerous
Syn. Burdensome, troublesome, wearing, oppressive, difficult.
Ant. Easy, unburdensome, harmless, comfortable, fluent.

Opening
Syn. Hole, eye, eyelet, slot, orifice, door, hatch, skylight, arcade, lattice, window, throat, sucker, mouth, vent, inlet, outlet, slit.
Ant. Close, closure, want, opportunity, purdah, screen shutter, shut off.

Operation

Syn. Action, effect, force, performance, influence, agency, executive, result, procedure.

Ant. Failure, inaction, uselessness, ineffectiveness, inefficiency, powerlessness.

Opinion

Syn. Thought, idea, bar, combat, contradict, counter, obstruct, contravene, check.

Ant. Aid, abet, befriend, encourage, help, assist, support.

Oppose

Syn. Resist, hinder, bar, combat, contradict, counter, obstruct, contravene, check.

Ant. Aid, abet, befriend, encourage, help, assist, support.

Optimist

Syn. Hopeful, confident, brave, bright, cheerful, happy.

Ant. Pessimist, dejected, drooping, disappointed, cheerless, hopeless.

Optional

Syn. Elective, non-obligatory, voluntary, discretionary.

Ant. Obligatory, enforced, compulsory.

Oral

Syn. Verbal, vocal, spoken.

Ant. Written, inscribed.

Order

Syn. Behest, injunction, mandate, requirement, prohibition, instruction, direction.

Ant. Allowance, consent, permit, permission, leave, liberty, licence.

Ordinary

Syn. Average, common, usual, commonplace, regular, unremarkable, medium, low, inferior, undistinguished.

Ant. Extraordinary, one in a million, uncommon, above the average, abnormal, high, first-rate, superiors, distinguished.

Organisation

Syn. Systmatisation, classification, association, co-ordination, set-up, society.

Ant. Misarrangement, pell-mell, unit, singleness, individual.

Origin

Syn. Beginning, cause, inception, foundation, derivation, source, root.

Ant. Result, issue, effect, sequel, outcome.

Ornament

Syn. Ornamentation, richness, tracery, beautification, adornment, powder, polish, paint, decoration, embellishment, lining.

Ant. Simplicity, unadornedness, plainess.

Over

Syn. Besides, additional, above, across, athwart.

Ant. Under, underneath, below, beneath.

Own

Syn. Have, hold, possess, admit, grant, acknowledge, concede.

Ant. Deny, lack, need, want, renounce, abjure, disavow, disclaim.

Pacify

Syn. Appease, mitigate, quell, lull, allay, compose, quiet, assuage, tranquillise, reconcile.

Ant. Irritate, inflame, annoy, incense, enrage, exasperate, vex.

Pain

Syn. Ache, distress, torment, woe, twinge, throe, pang, agony, anguish, grief.

Ant. Comfort, ease, peace, rapture, relief, delight, enjoyment, relief, pleasure.

Painting

Syn. Depicting, drawing, realism, tableau, watercolour, seascape, scene, still, life, panorama, classicism, romanicism.

Ant. Creation, construction, materialisation, building.

Pale

Syn. Cadaverous, ashy, wan, faint, pallid, light, colourless, sallow.

Ant. Dark, pitchy, dusky, swarthy, ebony.

Parcel

Syn. Pack, group, packet, load, bundle, allot, distribute, deal, mete, share, apportion, divide.

Ant. Collect, muster, collate, gather.

Pardon

Syn. Absolution, mercy, remission, oblivion, forbearance, amnesty, forgiveness, acquittal.

Ant. Penalty, retaliation, punishment, retribution, vengeance.

Pardon

Syn. Excuse, pass by, overlook, remit, pass over, forgive, acquit.

Ant. Castigate, chasten, visit, sentence, punish, doom, correct, condemn.

Parent
Syn. Father, mother, god-mother, guardian, paternity, maternity.
Ant. childhood.

Part
Syn. Atom, member, portion, share, segment, section, particle, fraction, fragment, piece, disconnect, disjoin.
Ant. Connect, join, tie, attach, link, combine, couple, cement.

Partial
Syn. Unfair, incomplete, limited, biased, interest, inequitable, restricted, predisposed, one-sided.
Ant. Fair, complete, entire, equitable, disinterested, whole, just, impartial, unprejudiced.

Particularly
Syn. Especially, distinctly, specially, chiefly.
Ant. Generally, vaguely, ordinarily.

Party
Syn. Side, club, sisterhood, caste, family, clique, bunch, ring, crew, mob, brotherhood.
Ant. Unit, independence, freedom, individual, individualism.

Pass
Syn. Proceed, exceed, slip, move, transcend, surpass, cease, die, lapse.
Ant. Last, continue, remain, abide, endure.

Passage
Syn. Transmission, flow, flight, stream, shipment, course, tract, vehicle, current, interpenetration, egress.
Ant. End, destiny, dead end, goal, terminus, destination.

Passion
Syn. Love, fervour, anger, fury, emotion, fever, intensify, desire, excitement.
Ant. Idea, conception, belief, thought.

Past
Syn. Preterition, yesterday, day of yore, yesteryear, syne, time, immemorial.
Ant. Future, coming time, tomorrow, coming events, to be.

Patience
Syn. Forbearance, passiveness, sufferance, resignation, edurance, fortitude, calmness.

Ant. Wrath, ire, rage, annoy, infuriate, vex, displease, inflame, incite, indignation, irritation, provoke.

Patient
Syn. Resigned, calm, suffering, passive, contented, uncomplaining, submissive.

Ant. Passionate, impetus, vehement.

Pause
Syn. Respite, interval, break, halt, cessation, intermission, lull, suspension, stoppage, wait.

Ant. Continuance, continuation, continue.

Pay
Syn. Allowance, fee, recompense, salary, stipend, wages, requital, payment, remuneration, hire, honorarium, emolument, earnings.

Payment
Syn. Defrayment, revenge, repayment, satisfaction, liquidation, discharge, settlement, clearance.

Ant. Receipt, debt, credit, non-payment, possession, attainment.

Peace
Syn. Harmony, repose, agreement, concord, calm, silence, tranquility.

Ant: Turmoil, was, discordance, dissonance, dissension, strife, contention.

Peculiar
Syn. Strange, extraordinary, remarkable, odd, queer, unusual, rare, abnormal, uncommon, irregular, singular.

Ant. Natural, customary, normal, commonplace, usual, ordinary.

Prefect
Syn. Finished, complete, whole, through, sound, spotless, accomplished

Ant. Imperfect, defective, incomplete, faulty.

Perfume
Syn. Fragrance, redolence, scent, incense, aroma.
Ant. Stench, fetid, stink, odour.

Perhaps
Syn. May be, probably, per chance, possibly.
Ant. Positively, surely, certainly.

Period
Syn. Era, age, time, term, season, span, cycle.
Ant. Endlessness, boundlessness, infinity, perpetuity.

Permeate
Syn. Overspread, saturate, fill, percolate, diffuse, pervade, penetrate.
Ant. Exude, ooze out.

Permission.
Syn. Allowance, authorisation, leave, licence, permit, liberty, authority.
Ant. Prevention, refusal, resistance, probibition, denial, hindrance, opposition, objection.

Persist
Syn. Continue, last, remain, stay, endure, insist, persevere.
Ant. Abstain, conclude, quit, give over, intermit, finish, terminate, end, desist, conclude, cease, discontinue.

Persuade
Syn. Allure, win, urge, over, lead, incite, entice, coax, convince, incline, move, induce, impel, bring over.
Ant. Hold back, restrain, deter, repel, dissuade, hinder, discourage.

Physical
Syn. Substantial, tangible, material, visible, corporeal.
Ant. Immaterial, incorporeal, spiritual, ethereal.

Pick
Syn. Glean, gather, cull, collect, select, extract, choose.
Ant. Reject, discard, exclude.

Piece
Syn. Portion, slice, scrap, shred, fragment, part, morsel, particle.
Ant. Whole, aggregate, sum, total, entirety.

Pitiable

Syn. Mounful, moving, grievous, distressing, sad, doleful, woeful, affecting, sorrowful.

Ant. Pleasant desirable, enviable.

Plant

Syn. Seed, set out, snow, seed down, set.

Ant. Weed out, uproot, eradicate extirpate.

Plead

Syn. Urge, solicit, advocate, ask, beseech, implore, press, entreat, beg, pray, sue, entreat.

Ant. Command, demand, order.

Pleasant

Syn. Delicious, gratifying, pleasing, welcome, pleasurable, kind, kindly, greteful,congenial, attractive, agreeable, acceptable, enjoyable.

Ant. Arrogant, unpleasant, unkind, repulsive, illhumored, horrible, harsh, distressing, grim, depressing, crabbed, austere, gloomy.

Plentiful

Syn. Abundant, lavish, replete, luxuriant, bountiful, ample, plenteous, teeming, sufficient.

Ant. Scarce, limited, niggardly, sparing, skimpy, scanty, insufficient.

Plenty

Syn. Exuberance, overflow, plentitude, abundance, profusion, copiousness.

Ant. Scarcity, want, infrequency, lack, insufficiency, storage, deficiency.

Poet

Syn. Bard, singer, rhymer, versifier, minstrel, troubadour, poetaster.

Poetry

Syn. Arts poetica, muse, pesy, prosody, rhyming, orthometry, rondo, triolet, libretto, jingle.

Ant. Prose, speech, article, talk.

Poison

Syn. Bane, venom, toxicity, virtue.

Ant. Honey, antidote, sweet, breed.

95

Polite

Syn. Accomplish, elegant, polished, urbane, genteel, gallant, courtly, courteous, civil, complaisant, chivalrous, cultivated.

Ant. Awkward, bluff, untaught, unpolished, uncouth, brusk, ill, bred, clownish, raw, insolent, insulting, discourteous, coarse.

Position

Syn. Post, place, bearing, attitude, station, site, locality, situation, posture, state, condition, circumstance, status, rank, standing, berth, job.

Ant. A triffle, non-existence, cipher, useless.

Positive

Syn. Definite, sure, actual, unequivocal.

Ant. Doubtful, indefinite, uncertain, equivocal, contestable.

Possess

Syn. Have, command, seize, own, hold, obtain, enjoy.

Ant. Want, forfeit, lose, need, disposses.

Possible

Syn. Likely, potential, conceivable, practicable, feasible.

Ant. Impossible, impracticable, unachievable, inconceivable.

Poverty

Syn. Beggary, need, penury, distress, privation, indigence, destitution, mendancy.

Ant. Riches, affluence, opulence, profusion, exuberance, plenty wealth.

Power

Syn. Ability, talent, command, skill, sway, strength, rule, might, force, potency, expertness, dexterity, efficacy, energy, cogency, capability, authority.

Ant. Unskilfulness, stupidity, helplessness, dullness, inaptitude, incapability, inability, incompetence, inefficiency, weakness.

Praise

Syn. Acclaim, flattery, plaudite, laudation, approval, cheers, cheering, compliment, applause, approbation.

Ant. Abuse, vituperation, slander, scorn, repudiation, obloquy, reproof, hissing, disparagement, contempt, blame, condemnation.

Prayer
Syn. Thanks giving, devotion, entreaty, request, worship, addoration.
Ant. Atheism, egotism, action, egoism, indifference, materialism.

Precious
Syn. Costly, valuable, inestimable, invaluable, prized, treasured
Ant. Cheap, worthless, despicable, valueless, useless, paltry.

Predominant
Syn. Over-ruling, prominent, superior, dominant, ruling, controlling, prevalent.
Ant. Minor, inferior, unimportant, junior, petty, subsidiary, subordinate.

Predicament
Syn. Plight, puzzle, strait, fix, difficulty, jam, perplexity.
Ant. Assurance, self-satisfaction, rest, decision, ease, comfort, confidence, content, calmness, certainty.

Prediction
Syn. Announcement, prophecy, forecast, augury, foreboding, warning, fortune-telling, foresight, divination.
Ant. Mystery, secrecy, hiding, occult, concealment.

Prejudice
Syn. Unfairness, presumption, preconception, bias, partiality.
Ant. Certainty, reasoning, conviction, demonstration, evidence, proof, reason, reasoning.

Premature
Syn. Rash, unreasonable, previous, early, precipitate, untimely.
Ant. Delayed, reasonable, overdue, late, slow.

Present
Syn. Donation, gift, largesse, offer, bestow, introduce, give, grant, deliver, hand, exhibit, offering, gratuity.
Ant. Forfeit, forfeiture, loss, keep back, restrain.

Press
Syn. Harass, force, crush, compel, squeeze, crowd, constrain, squash, compress, force.
Ant. Pull, relax, deter, hold back, impede, loosen, slacken.

Pressure
Syn. Influence, stress, compulsion, exigency, force, hurry, urgency.
Ant. Relaxation, slackening.

Pretend
Syn. Fabricate, sham, feign, simulate, profess, allege, counterfeit.
Ant. Verify, substantiate, establish, authenticate.

Pretty
Syn. Beautiful, comely, lovely, charming.
Ant. Ugly, unlovely, uncomely, hideous, ungainly.

Prevailing
Syn. Predominant, dominant, preponderating, controlling.
Ant. Impotent, subsidiary, subordinate, powerless, ineffective.

Prevent
Syn. Obviate, preclude, forestall, anticipate.
Ant. Help, aid, abet, further, second, back.

Previous
Syn. Aforesaid, anterior, former, prior, precedent, preceding, antecedent, foregoing.
Ant. Succeeding, hindmost, later, latter, consequent, following, hind, concluding.

Priceless
Syn. Invaluable, inestimable.
Ant. Cheap, nexpensive.

Pride
Syn. Ego, haughtiness, vanity, hauteur, self-esteem, self-importance, self-respect, dignity.
Ant. Goodness, gentleness, humility, meekness.

Principal
Syn. Capital, surpassing, first, main prime, prevailing, foremost, highest, chief, controlling, prominent, superior, pre-eminent.
Ant. Accessory, added, additional, inferior, supplemental, minor, negligible, secondary, helping, inconsiderable.

Prison
Syn. Jail, gaol, coop, den, cell, keep, dungeon, lock up, singe, house of correction.
Ant. Liberty, libertinism, the great world, open field.

Privacy
Syn. Secrecy, solitude, seclusion, concealment.
Ant. Spotlight, advertisement, propaganda, publicity.

Privilege
Syn. Favour, charter, grant, licence, immunity, exemption, right, prerogative.
Ant. Inhibition, veto, interdictment, prohibition, debarment.

Probable
Syn. Credible, possible, likely.
Ant. Certainly, surely, questionably, positively, definitely.

Production.
Syn. Formation, construction, creation, operation, achievement, bringing forth, coinage, edification, workmanship.
Ant. Destruction, consumption, pulling, down, decay, death, end, waste.

Profit
Syn. Advantage, gain, good, improvement, returns, value, utility, service, receipts, benefit, proceeds, expediency.
Ant. Damage, destruction, waste, ruin, loss, injury, hurt, harm, disadvantage, detriment.

Progress
Syn. Advance, growth, increase, progression improvement. development, attainment.
Ant. Decline, delay, stop, stay, falling off, stoppage, retrogression.

Prohibit
Syn. Ban, prevent, preclude, inhibit, hinder, disallow, debar, forbid, interdict.
Ant. Authorise, consent to, direct, suffer, tolerate, warrant, order, permit, give consent, enjoin, empower, command, allow.

Prolong

Syn. Lengthen, continue, protract, extend, stretch, sustain, quicken, accelerate.

Ant. Contain, lessen, shorten, diminish, abridge, decrease, contract, abbreviate, delay.

Prominent

Syn. Conspicuous, distinctive, marked, celebrated, distinguished, leading, eminent, notable, principal.

Ant. Inconspicuous, minor, junior, unimportant, petty.

Promise

Syn. Truth, undertaking, pledge, parole, word of honour, vow, oath, obligation, affiance, betrothal, contract.

Ant. Non-commitment, want of firmness, promiselessness, non-assurance.

Promote

Syn. Lengthen, continue, protract, extend, stretch, sustain, quicken, accelerate.

Ant. Contain, lessen, shorten, diminish, abridge, decrease, contract, abbreviate, abbreviate, delay.

Property

Syn. Possession, lordship, ownership, empire, demand, dominion, right, title, trust, free, tail, tenure, estate, proprietorship.

Ant. Dispossession, landlessness, havenotness, poverty.

Proposal

Syn. Bid, offer, proposition, motion, overture, suggestion.

Ant. Non-acceptance, denial, disapproval, refusal, rejection, repulse.

Prophet

Syn. Foreteller, palmist, holyman, star-gazer, forecaster, reformer, saint, astrologer.

Ant. Follower, misleader, ignorant, person, devil.

Prosperity

Syn. Progress, windfall, luck, fat years, palmy days, sunshine, good fortune, fair weather, welfare, wealth, wellbeing.

Ant. Misfortune, evil days, poverty, adversity, misery.

Portect

Syn. Shield, harbour, cover, defend, save, guard, shelter, fortify, preserve.

Ant. Unmask, exhibit, reveal, disclose, denounce, expose, uncover.

Protest

Syn. Remonstration, declaration, expostulate, asseverate, declare, affirm, object, assertion.

Ant. Permission, sanction, acquiesce, abet, countenance, aid, allowance, assist, encourage.

Proud

Syn. Arrogant, lofty, stately, conceited, haughty, egotistical, supercilious.

Ant. Humble, modest, lowly, unpretentious, unpretending, unassuring.

Prove

Syn. Attest, justify, verify, demonstrate, establish, show, confirm.

Ant. Refuse, negative, deny, confute, disprove.

Provide

Syn. Supply, prepare, furnish, get, arrange, cater, procure, purvey.

Ant. Consume, spend, expend, dissipate, exhaust, use.

Prudence

Syn. Wisdom, discertain, care, discrimination, foresight, judiciousness, knowledge, sharpness, wit, carefulness, tact.

Ant. Foolishness, carelessness, wastfulness, thoughtlessness.

Public

Syn. Popular, open, published, general, common, national, known.

Ant. Private, unofficial, clandestine, privy, personal, concealed.

Publish

Syn. Proclaim, disclose, disseminate, advertise, declare, divulage, promulgate, broadcast, announce.

Ant. Suppress, extinguish, smother, repress, conceal, check, cloak, stifle, restrain.

Punctual

Syn. Prompt, timely, exact.

Ant. Late, tardy, slack, loitering, unpunctual, dilatory.

Punish
Syn. Afflict, chasten, subdue, humble, chastise, correct, discipline, castigate.
Ant. Recompense, indemnity, reward, repay, compensate, remuneration.

Purchase
Syn. Acquire, secure, procure, get, obtain, buy, bargain for, barter for.
Ant. Sell, put to sale, exchange, dispose of.

Pure
Syn. Guiltless, spotless, simple, unmixed, virtuous, upright, unsullied, true, immaculate, incorrupt, mere, perfect, real, sheer, absolute, chaste, classic, clean, clear, genuine.
Ant. Adulterted, defiled, dirty, unclean, unchaste, trained, sullied, gross, foul, filthy, mixed, lewd, indelicate.

Purpose
Syn. Aim, object, plan, intention, end, meaning, resolve, intent.
Ant. Accident, chance, hazard, vague, meaningless, aimless.

Pursuit
Syn. Prosecution, enterprise, occupation, avocation, vocation, hue and cry, profession, business, undertaking.
Ant. Idleness, worklessness, tedium, unemployment, boredom.

Push
Syn. 'Press, thrust, shove, jostle, urge, drive, propel, impel.
Ant. Pull, haul, drag, tow, tug.

Quality
Syn. Excellence, property, brand, nature, status, trait, characteristic, attribute, colouring, gentility.
Ant. Quantity, flatness, commonness, colourlessness.

Quantity
Syn. Measure, amount, bulk, number, sum-total, volume, aggregate.
Ant. Shortage, deficiency, insufficiency, deficit.

Quarrel
Syn. Wrangle, affray, contention, contest, enmity, hostility, fight, riot, row, strife, fracas, controversy, brawl.
Ant. Agreement, assent, consent, acquiesce, harmony, friendship, peace, amity, equanimity, concord, accede, agree.

Queer
Syn. Eccentric, abnormal, strange, odd, curious, peculiar, extraordinary, unusual, singular, strange, fantastic.
Ant. Ordinary, habitual, everyday, normal, common, usual, commonplace.

Question
Syn. Doubt, query, investigation, interrogation, inquiry, interogatory, inquisition.
Ant. Reply, answer, rejoinder, respond, rejoin, response.

Quicken
Syn. Hasten, urge, speed, make-haste, further, drive, advance, accelerate, expedite, drive on, dispatch.
Ant. Check, obstruct, retard, drag, hinder, impede, delay.

Quickness
Syn. Velocity, celerity, haste, fleetness, rapidity, swiftness.
Ant. Slowness, sluggishness, inertia.

Quiet

Syn. Respose, stillness, compose, lull, mollify, calm, soothe, still, allay, appease, hush, calmness, quietude, rest.

Ant. Excitement, tumult, commotion, turmoil, exasperate, disturb, aggravate, disquiet, enhance.

Quite

Syn. Completely, precisely, utterly, totally, wholly, entirely, altogether, fully.

Ant. Partially, partly, incompletely.

R

Race
Syn. Tribe, people, family, caste, nation, ethic, group.
Ant. Unit, individual, humanity, mankind, generation, global, brotherhood.

Racy
Syn. Flavorous, rich, spicy, spirited, poignant, lively.
Ant. Cold, vapid, dull, flat, stale, prosy, insipid, tasteless, stupid.

Radical
Syn. Basal, basic, complete, entire, essential, native, extreme, natural, primitive, thorough, total, perfect, positive, innate.
Ant. Trial, tentative, inadequate, conservative, partial, slight, superficial.

Raid
Syn. Pillage, inroad, forage, plunder, invade, assault, invasion.
Ant. Peaceful, timidity, cowardice.

Rapidity
Syn. Velocity, speed, despatch, haste, celerity, quickness, swiftness.
Ant. Slowness, inertia.

Rare
Syn. Curious, odd, peculiar, scarce, unique, infrequent, remarkable, unusual, uncommonly, precious, unparalled, incomparable.
Ant. Common, usual, frequent, familiar, hackneyed, customary, trite.

Rash
Syn. Hasty, venturesome, foolhardy, indiscreet, dareless, reckless, precipitate, incautious.
Ant. Careful, wary, discrete, cautious.

Rashness
Syn. Imprudence, recklessness, foolhardiness, heedlessness, indiscretion.
Ant. Care, caution, penny-wisdom, prudence, thoughtfulness.

Rate
Syn. Appraise, compute, estimate, reckon, assess, price.
Ant. Miscalculate, under-rate, under-value.

Ratio
Syn. Proportion, rate, comparison, degree, percentage.
Ant. Centpercent, unproportioned, peerless.

Ration
Syn. Allotment, quota, part, port, portion, share.
Ant. Totality, aggregate, entirety, entirety, whole, sum-total.

Reach
Syn. Arrive, land, gain, enter, attain, come to.
Ant. Start, set sail, set out, go away, depart, embark.

Readiness
Syn. Promptitude, willingness, eagerness, alacrity, quickness.
Ant. Unwillingness, reluctance, reluctance, disinclination, aversion, tardiness.

Real
Syn. Actual, demonstrable, genuine, true, positive, developed, veritable, essential, certain.
Ant. Conceived, reported, visionary, untrue, unreal, imaginary, fiction, fanciful, illusory.

Reason
Syn. Rationalism, thinking, logic, analysis, exposition, generalisation.
Ant. Illogicality, stupidity, nonsense, senselessness, foolishness.

Rebellion
Syn. Sedition, mutiny, uprising, insurrection, revolt.
Ant. Loyalty, patriotism, devotion, faithfulness, nationalism, toadyism.

Rebuke
Syn. Censure, admonish, chide, rebuff, up-braid, reprehend, reprimand.
Ant. Acclaim, compliment, applaud, praise, laud.

Receive
Syn. Get, take, accept, welcome, meet, greet, derive, entertain.
Ant. Give, grant, bestow, donate, supply, contribute, present.

Reconsider
Syn. Review, amend, overhaul, re-survey, alter, re-examine.
Ant. Inferred, cònclusion, judgement, induction.

Record
Syn. Register, roll, story, monument, memorial, history, entry, enrollment, account, archive, document, inscription.
Ant. Smother, repress, conceal, suppress.

Recover
Syn. Healed, restored, recruit, repossess, retrieve, regain, restore, resume, cure.
Ant. Die, sink, worse, grow, fail, replace.

Reduce
Syn. Curtail, lower, debase, diminish, contract, mitigate, decrease, lessen, attenuate, abate, shorten, degrade.
Ant. Increase, raise, promote, augment, enhance, dignity, extol, ennoble, intensify, enlarge.

Refresh
Syn. Cheer, strengthen, invigorate, brace, exhilarate, freshen, revive.
Ant. Tire, fag, jade, weary, exhaust.

Refund
Syn. Repay, restore, reimburse, return.
Ant. Keep, withhold, detain, reserve, suppress.

Refuse
Syn. Veto, renounce, withhold, decline, exclude, deny, repudiate.
Ant. Acquiesce, agree, grant, cede, admit, accede, allow, give, consent.

Regain
Syn. Recapture, recover, retrieve, repossess.
Ant. Lose, forfeit, mislay.

Regal
Syn. Stately, kingly, grand, imperial, princely.
Ant. Ignoble, mean, lowly, common, ordinary.

Regarding
Syn. Touching about, referring, respecting.
Ant. Omitting, overlooking, disregarding, ignoring.

Rejoice
Syn. Delight, revel, glory, exult.
Ant. Mourn, sorrow, lament, bewail, grieve.

Relation
Syn. Bearing, affinity, interest, kin, reference, kinship.
Ant. difference, enmity, hostility, disaffiliation, dissociation.

Release
Syn. Disentangle, exempt, liberate, unloose, relive, free, disengage, extricate, emancipate.
Ant. Bind, confine, enthrall, restrain.

Religion
Syn. Church, theology, faith, sect, creed, communion, denomination, persuasion.
Ant. Atheism, wickedness, unbelief, sacrilege, irreligion, godlessness, impiety.

Reluctant
Syn. Disinclined, unwilling, averse, slow, opposed, indisposed, backward.
Ant. Desirous, inclined, willing, eager, disposed, favourable.

Remark
Syn. Regard, utter, say, observe, comment, note, declare, express, heed.
Ant. Miss, disregard, overlook.

Remarkable
Syn. Extraordinary, conspicuous, striking, famous, noticeable strange, distinguish.
Ant. Ordinary, commonplace, customary, normal, average, habitual, medium.

Remember
Syn. Recollect, recall.
Ant. Overlook, forget.

Remorse
Syn. Compunction, penitence, repentance, sorrow, contrition.
Ant. Gratification, contentment, satisfaction, pleasure.

Renounce
Syn. Abandon, deny, revoke, retract, refuse, reject, disavow, disclaim, abjure, foreswear, repudiate.
Ant. Uphold, avow, adopt, assert, proclaim, own, hold, defend, maintain, claim, cherish.

Repair
Syn. Make, patch up, restore, mend, make, amends.
Ant. Mar, damage, injure, hurt, spoil, break.

Repeal
Syn. Abolish, recall, revoke, nullify, reverse, annul, rescind.
Ant. Substantiate, ratify, endorse, confirm, assent.

Repeat
Syn. Reiterate, reproduce, relate, narrate, cite, echo, rehearse, double, duplicate.
Ant. Suppress, recant, renounce, conceal, repudiate.

Repentance
Syn. Contrition, regret, compunction, sorrow, penitence, grief.
Ant. Satisfaction, complacency, pleasure, gratification.

Replace
Syn. Substitute, rehabilitate, restore, reinstate, refund.
Ant. Discharge, transplant, displace, remove, dislodge, expel.

Reproach
Syn. Upbraid, reprove, blame, obloquy, disapprobation reprimand, dishonour, censure, chide, rebuke.
Ant. Praise, exaltation, honour, exalt, applaud, comment, commend, dignify, encomium.

Repulse
Syn. Repel, rebuff, check, reject.
Ant. Encourage, promote, allow, advance, abet, further, permit, foster.

Rescue
Syn. Deliver, recover, redeem, save, liberate, release.
Ant. Hazard, risk, imperil, jeoparadise, endanger.

Resent
Syn. Take ill, dislike, hate, detest, take, offence at..
Ant. Relish, like, love, esteem.

Resident
Syn. Inhabitant, dweller, tenant, occupant.
Ant. Guest, caller, visitor, bird-of-passage.

Resign
Syn. Renounce, yield, abandon, quit, leave, surrender, abdicate.
Ant. Hold, stay, continue, remain, maintain, retain, keep.

Respectable
Syn. Reputable, estimable, decent, honourable, fair, worthy.
Ant. Disreputable, unworthy, sordid, despicable, base, dishonourable.

Responsible
Syn. Answerable, liable, amenable, accountable.
Ant. Absolute, unlimited, unfettered, unconditioned, free, supreme, arbitary.

Rest
Syn. Respose, peacefulness, tranquility, feast, holiday, peace.
Ant. Work, exertion, restlessness, worry, anxiety, disturbance.

Result
Syn. Issue, effect, decision, upshot, end, consequence, outcome.
Ant. Origin, cause, reason, source, agent.

Retain
Syn. Employ, engage, maintain, keep, hold.
Ant. Give up, cede, surrender, relinquish, renounce, forsake, abandon.

Retire
Syn. Fall back, shrink, retreat, withdraw, depart, recede.
Ant. Push forward, advance, march, progress.

Return
Syn. Come back, remit, recompence, revert, recur, restore.
Ant. Vanish, disappear.

Revenge
Syn. Vengeance, requital, avenging, retaliation.
Ant. Compassion, pity, grace, mercy, reconciliation, pardon.

Revengeful
Syn. spiteful, vengeful, merciless, resentful, vindictive.
Ant. Forgiving, kind, humane, element, benign, forbearing, merciful.

Reverse
Syn. Failure. misfortune, affliction, defect, hardship, overturn, capsize, invert, subvert, up end.
Ant. Success, prosperity, victory, triumph, reinstate, restore.

Reward
Syn. Prize, award reparation, satisfaction, recompense, retribution, requital, amends.
Ant. Punish, penalise, chasten, penalty, punishment, fine, discipline.

Rhythm
Syn. Meter, verse, euphony, measure.
Ant. Disagreeable, in sound, inharmonious.

Riddle
Syn. Mystery, puzzle, problem, paradox, enigma, conundrum.
Ant. Answer, explanation, solution, proposition, axiom.

Right
Syn. Lawful, straight, true, rightful, just, good, honest, fitting, correct, direct, fair, proper, unswerving.
Ant. Bad, crooked, incorrect, false, unjust, unrighteous, wrong, iniquitous, unfair.

Right
Syn. Licence, prerogative, privilege, liberty, claim, franchise, immunity, perquisite.

Riot
Syn. Orgy, excess, revelry, outbreak, lawessness, commotion, disorder, unpoar, disturbance.
Ant. Order, abstinence, law, peace, sobrity, temperance, tranquility.

Rise
Syn. Emanate, flow, proceed, spring, ascend, arise, issue.
Ant. Drop, fall, go down, set, settle, decline, sink, descent.

Risk
Syn. Hazard, jeoparadise, venture, peril, danger, imperil, stake, endanger.
Ant. Security, secure, save, harbour, safety, defend, shelter, shield.

Roam
Syn. Rove, saunter, ramble, prowl, wander, meander, range.
Ant. Hurry, haste, hasten.

Roar
Syn. Thunder, yell, shout, peal, bellow, boom, vociferate, resound.
Ant. Dull, in slow manner, peacefully, silently.

Rob
Syn. Divest, embezzle, pilfer, deprive, dispossess, denude, plunder, steal, strip.
Ant. Enrich, endow, supply.

Rogue
Syn. Miscreant, cheat, scoundrel, rascal, knave, villain, swindler, scamp.
Ant. Gentleman.

Room
Syn. Scope, boudoir, apartment, field, latitude, range, compass, expanse.
Ant. Limitation, restriction.

Round
Syn. Globular, circular, spherical.
Ant. Angular, craggy, sharp-corned.

Rub
Syn. Scour, smooth, smear, abrade, chafe, grate, polish, clean, wipe, grave.
Ant. To draw, image, picture, to write upon.

Rude
Syn. Discourteous, impudent, unmannerly, saucy, churlish, impertinent, impolite.
Ant. Civil, cultivate, polished, courteous, elegant, genteel, refined.

Ruin
Syn. Subvert, shatter, desolate, destroy, crush, wreck, defeat, demolish.

Ant. Save, redeem, extricate, rescue, recover.

Ruin
Syn. Destruction, desolation, subversion, undoing, prostration, collapse, downfall, havoc.

Ant. Compensation, restoration, reparation, repair.

Ruling
Syn. Controlling, reigning, prevailing, common, predominant, usual, governing.

Ant. Unusual, exception, rare, infrequent, uncommon.

Rumour
Syn. Report, gossip, common talk, heresy, scandal, story, tale.

Ant. Truth, fact.

Rural
Syn. Simple, countrified, pastoral, sylvan, rustic, clownish.

Ant. Urban, civic, metropolitan.

Rustic
Syn. Verdant, sylvan, rural, rude, countrified, coarse, country, boorish, awkward, artless, agricultural, uncouth, plain.

Ant. Accomplished, well-bred, polished, polite, citylike, cultured, urban, refined.

S

Sacred
Syn. Holy, sanctified, dedicated, consecrated, inviolable, hallowed.
Ant. Profane, impious, irreverent, irreligious, blasphemous, sacrilegious.

Sad
Syn. Grave, woeful, sober, gloomy, dismal, despondent, depressed, heavy, sombre, sorry, unhappy, distressiing, doleful, miserable, sorrowful.
Ant. Cheerful, joyous, buoyant, merry, happy, joyful, gay, jocund, blithsome, mirthful, gleeful, glad.

Safe
Syn. Secure, fear-free, impregnable, sure, confident.
Ant. Unsafe, afraid, insecure, vulnerable, pregnable.

Safety
Syn. Defence, protection, safeguard, security.
Ant. Insecurity, peril, uncertainty.

Sailor
Syn. Mariner, seaman, wind jammer, blue jacket, seafarer.
Ant. Land-lubber, factory-worker, porter, coaster, millhand.

Same
Syn. Like, ditto, corresponding, similar, identical, analogous.
Ant. Unlike, deviating, divergent, different, dissimilar.

Sample
Syn. Case, illustration, specimen, instance, exemplification.
Ant. Abnormality, aggregate, exception, monstrosity, whole, total.

Sanction
Syn. Allow, support, approve, ratify, endorse, authorise, permit, confirm.
Ant. Disallow, debar, veto, ban, interdict, forbid, prohibit.

Satisfy
Syn. Glut, satiate, fill, surfeit, content.
Ant. Check, tantalise, refuse, restrict, straighten, stint, starve, disappoint, refuse.

Say
Syn. Express, declare, utter, speak, pronounce, tell, assert, allege.
Ant. Suppress, conceal, repress.

Scanty
Syn. Narrow, skimpy, pinched, sparing, slender, meagre, limited, small.
Ant. Profuse, abundant, lavish, unlimited, sufficient, ample, copious.

Scatter
Syn. Sprinkle, disperse, spread, broadcast, propagate, dissipate, distribute, disseminate.
Ant. Hoard, gather, husband, store, collect, amass, pick, garner, accumulate.

Scholar
Syn. Disciple, student, pendant, savant, fellow, learner, pupil.
Ant. Dunce, illiterate person, fool, ignoramous, idiot, idler.

Science
Syn. Erudition, lore, knowledge, learning, technical, skill, technology, mechanical, efficiency.
Ant. Data, philosophy, uncoordinated knowledge, fiction, imagination, nature study.

Scold
Syn. Reprimand, censure, reprove, chide, rebuke, admonish.
Ant. Compliment, applaud, praise, commend.

Scorn
Syn. Slight, disregard, deride, sneer, disdian, derision, ridicule, contempt.
Ant. Revere, respect, regard, defence, esteem.

Search
Syn. Examine, hunt, investigate, inquiry, research, quest, investigation, explore, probe.
Ant. Ignore, conjecture, supposition, surmise, guess, fancy, suppose.

Seasonable
Syn. Suitable, appropriate, timely, opportune, proper.
Ant. Unsuitable, unreasonable, inappropriate, inopportune, unfit.

Secrecy
Syn. Concealment, seclusion, obscurity, solitude, retirement.
Ant. Spotlight, notoriety, publicity.

Secret
Syn. Mystery, sealed book, nut to crack, jigsaw, esoteric, occult, labyrinth, sphinx.
Ant. Open secret, open book, published fact.

Seed
Syn. Origin, source, progency, offspring, children, embryo, germ, descendant, original.
Ant. Issue, predecessors, forefathers, outcome, product, result, progenitors, ancestors.

Seek
Syn. Hunt, court, inquire for, look for, search, solicit, follow, ask.
Ant. Shun, avoid, eschew, evade.

Seldom
Syn. Rarely, hardly, ever, occasionally.
Ant. Often repeatedly, frequently.

Selfish
Syn. Sordid, greedy, mercenary, ungenerous, illiberal, mean.
Ant. Generous, liberal, charitable, bountiful, lavish.

Sell
Syn. Vend, retail, dispose of, peddle, hawk, undo.
Ant. Buy, purchase.

Send
Syn. Transmit, project, hurl, drive, depute, discharge, emit, propel, dismiss, fling, lance, impel, delegate.
Ant. Bring, carry, keep, receive, retain, get, hand, hold, convey.

Sensibility
Syn. Susceptibility, feelings, impressibility, sensitiveness.
Ant. Coldness, deadness, unconsciousness, numbness, hardness.

Sensible
Syn. Judicious, wise, aware, conscious, observant, intelligent, sane, rational, sagacious, cognisant.
Ant. Unaware, senseless, idiotic, stupid, asinine, foolish, unconscious, senseless, doltish.

Sensual
Syn. Libidinous, prurient, carnal, lustful, lewd, licentious, lecherous, fleshy.
Ant. Sober, abstemious, anchorite, puritanical, restrained.

Separate
Syn. Divorce, disunite, divide, sever, disconnect, segregate, detach.
Ant. Unite, combine, conjoin, fasten, together, couple, cement, solder, connect.

Seperated
Syn. Disconnected, divided, dissociated, independent, detached, severed, unconnected, segregated.
Ant. Joined, connected, combined, associated, attached, united, welded, coupled.

Servant
Syn. Servitor, helper, jobber, subject, help, menial, retainer, flunkey, footman, livery, orderly, waiter.
Ant. Master, captain, director, employer, boss, commander, slave-owner.

Settle
Syn. Conclude, establish, fix, colonize, liquidate, finish, meet, domicile, people, adjust, decide, determine, discharge.
Ant. Ruffle, disconnect, confuse, derange, disorder.

Several
Syn. Many, manifold, diverse, sundry, various, numerous.
Ant. Few, scarce, scanty.

Severe

Syn. Austere, inexorable, inflexible, rigorous, stern, uncompromising, unmitigating, unyielding, hard, harsh, rigid, stiff.

Ant. Mild, lenient, yielding, gentle, easy, bland, affable, soft, pliable, tender, sweet.

Shadow

Syn. Shade, tail, umbra, reflection, sleuth.

Ant. Sunshine, brightness, truth, reality.

Shake

Syn. Agitate, waver, thrill, totter, reel, rock, brandish, flap, jolt, bounce, flutter, quake, quiver, swing, sway, shiver, tremble.

Ant. Stiffen, petrify, gell, coagulate, harden, nerve, strengthen.

Shallow

Syn. Trifling, superficial, superficial, slight, trivial, foolish, unintelligent, simple.

Ant. Wise, intelligent, shrewd, astute, dicerning, deep, recondite, clever.

Shame

Syn. Disgrace, modesty, dishonour, shyness, abashment, mortification, coyness.

Ant. Honour, fame, cuteness, impudence, freedom, courage, flare.

Shameless

Syn. Indecent, wanton, brazen, unashamed, unabashed, immodest, indelicate.

Ant. Modest, virtuous, decent.

Shave

Syn. Clip, skim, pare, shear, crop, slice.

Ant. Totatility, entire, complete.

Shelter

Syn. Guard, protect, screen, harbour, defend, shield.

Ant. Betray, cast out, expel, reject, surrender, refuse, expose.

Shine

Syn. Brightness, lustre, sheen, sparkle, glitter, glisten, glow, shimmer, polish, beam.

Ant. Tarnish, pale, fade, wane, dull, dullness.

Shock
Syn. Apeal, scare, dismay, offend, outrage, blow, collision, tremor, clash, disgust, stern, horrify.
Ant. Delight, gladden, please.

Show
Syn. Parade, display, pomp, prove, demonstration.
Ant. Cover, hide, mask, veil, suppress.

Showy
Syn. Sumptuous, magnificent, splendid, grand.
Ant. Colourless, simple, sombre.

Shrewd
Syn. Artful, astute, keen, subtle, sharp, knowing, discerning, crafty, penetrating, perspicacious.
Ant. Blind, dull, unintelligent, stupid, stolid, shortsighted, undiscerning.

Shy
Syn. Coy, diffident, timorous, timid, retiring, reassuming, reserved, shrinking.
Ant. Confident, assuming audacious, shameless, bold.

Sick
Syn. Indisposed, disordered, ill, diseased, poorly, unwell.
Ant. Well, healthy, hale, sound.

Sick
Syn. Disgusted, tired, weary.
Ant. Lively, playfulness, delighted

Side
Syn. Interest, cause, border, edge, party, flank, faction, sect.
Ant. Middle, centre.

Signify
Syn. Denote, intimate, foreshadow, mean show, proclaim, indicate.
Ant. Veil, mask, dissemble, cloak, cover, hide, conceal.

Silence
Syn. Noiselessness, dumbness, dullness, lull, quiet, quietness, stillness.
Ant. Talk, talkative, shrillness, sound, noisiness, noise.

Silly

Syn. Absurd, senseless, foolish, unwise, non-sensical.

Ant. Sensible, clever, wise, sapient, intelligent.

Similar

Syn. Alike, resembling, corresponding, homologous, analogous, congruous.

Ant. Differing, different, dissimilar, deviating, divergent.

Simple

Syn. Pure, clear, plain, modest, chaste, ordinary, bald, flat, dull, unadorned, unaffected, homely.

Ant. Complex, pretentious, arty, adorned, affected, fashionable.

Sin

Syn. Crime, wrong-doing, iniquity offence, misdeed, vice, wrong, wickdness, evil, criminality, ill-doing, injustice.

Ant. Blamelessness, excellence, right, virtue, purity, sinlessness, righteousness, integrity, holiness.

Sing

Syn. Carol, hum, warble, chant.

Ant. Weep, exude, exudate.

Single

Syn. individual, bachelor, unmarried, separate, sole, solitary, isolate.

Ant. Married, wedded, duat, escorted accompanied, numerous.

Size

Syn. Volume, width, breadth, extent, dimension, largeness, length, greatness.

Ant. Shapless, unmeasured, unmachanic, disorganised, uniform.

Skeptic

Syn. Agnostic, atheist, deist, doubter, infidel, unbeliever, disbeliever.

Ant. Trustful, superseding, supersedere.

Skilful

Syn. Competent, ingenious, adroit, clever, experienced.

Ant. Inexperienced, bungling, incompetent, clumsy, awkward.

Skill

Syn. Expertness, adroitness, knack, cleverness, ingenuity, dexterity.

Ant. Awkwardness, clumsiness.

Slander
Syn. Decry, defame, aspersion, calumny, opprobrium, accuse, malign, disparge, vilify, obloquy, defamation, asperse, traduce.
Ant. Praise, eulogium, panegyrise, applaud, eulogise, encomium commendation, laud, laudation, commend.

Slavery
Syn. Subjection, thraldom, bondage, forced, labour, submission, drudgery, servitude, captivity, subjugation.
Ant. Freedom, emancipation, liberty, independence.

Sleep
Syn. Slumber, coma, hypnosis, nap, doze, rest, somnolence, repose.
Ant. Wakefulness, sleeplessness, activity, vigilance.

Sleepy
Syn. Sluggish, lethargic, slumbrous, drowsy, somnolent, torpid, heavy.
Ant. Wakeful, animated, alert, energetic, active.

Slope
Syn. Descent, incline, ramp, gradient, acclivity, slant, declivity.
Ant. Flush, level, flat.

Slow
Syn. Tardy, slack, inert, drowsy, dull, laggard, gradual, inactive, deliberate, leisurely, delaying.
Ant. Active, quick, brisk, fast, fleet, prompt, alert, speedy, expeditious.

Smart
Syn. Spruce, trim, elegant, well-dressed, immaculate, neat, showy.
Ant. Ragged, worn, untidy, shabby, unkempt, threadbare.

Smart
Syn. Clever, agile, nimble, alert, sprightly, active.
Ant. Dull, stolid, doltish, slow, sluggish.

Smash
Syn. Disrupt, break, crack, shatter, crush.
Ant. Mend, rectify, restore, repair.

Smile
Syn. Grin, favour, look with ridicule, sneer, simper, smirk.
Ant. Sob, weep, cry, sigh, moan.

Smooth
Syn. Uniform, tranquillise, appease, sleek, plain, assuage, ally, polished, solace, mitigate.
Ant. Spindly, shaggy, ruffle, disquiet, provoke, incense, exasperate, uneven, bristly, irritate, torment.

Sneer
Syn. Scoff, flout, taunt, smile, deride, jeer.
Ant. Appreciate, thank, cheer, command.

Soak
Syn. Macerate, moisten, damp, saturate, wet.
Ant. Descicate, dry, dehydrate.

Sober
Syn. Temperate, abstinent, abstemious.
Ant. Intemperate, drunk, inebriated, intoxicated, tipsy.

Sober
Syn. Staid, solemn, calm, dispassionate, sedate, sane, serious, subdue, composed, grave.
Ant. Frivolous, flippant, thoughtless, reckless.

Sociable
Syn. Companionable, festive, friendly, affiliable, genial convivial.
Ant. Secluded, inimical, hostile, sequestered, foolish, puerile, giddy.

Socialism
Syn. Collectivism, welfare state, public ownership, communism.
Ant. Capitalism, non-communism, private, ownership, individualism.

Society
Syn. Company, companionship, aristocracy, folk, culture, club, group, association, elite, humanity.
Ant. Loneliness, seclusion, one-in-all, quietude.

Soft
Syn. Plastic, flexible, pliable, yielding, malleable, supple.
Ant. Hard, firm, unyielding, compact, rigid, stiff.

Soft

Syn. Amenable, tractable, gentle, tender, meek, lenient, compaliant, placid, mild.

Ant. Unkind, harsh, austere, churlish, stern, hard.

Soil

Syn. Mud, loam, earth, mould.

Soil

Syn. Begrime, stain, spoil, dirty, smear, pollute, taint, contaminate, sully.

Ant. Clarify, clean, purge, wash, cleanse, purify.

Solemn

Syn. Ceremonial, devotional, pious, irreligious, irreverent.

Ant. Impious, irreligious.

Solemn

Syn. Grave, sober, awe-inspiring, staid, funeral, sedate, august.

Ant. Jolly, cheerful, jovial, gay, sprightly, blithe, joyous, joy.

Solid

Syn. Compact, impenetrable, substantial, hard, firm, strong, dense, massive, weighty.

Ant. Soft, rarefied, hollow.

Solid

Syn. Sound, safe, reliable, trustworthy.

Ant. Unreliable, undependable, untrustworthy, unsafe.

Solitary

Syn. Unfrequented, unihabited, secluded, lonely, isolated, sequestered, deserted.

Ant. Habited, popular, frequented, public, society.

Solitary

Syn. Companionless, alone, lone, sole, lonely, lonesome.

Ant. accompanied

Solution

Syn. Disunion, liquefaction, disintegration, dissolution

Ant. Union, petrifaction, solidification, consolidation, crystallisation.

Solution
Syn. Key, explanation, answer.
Ant. Puzzle, question.

Soon
Syn. Shortly, quickly, presently, early.
Ant. Afterwards, subsequently, later.

Soothe
Syn. Palliate, alleviate, ease, appease, solace, assuage, calm, deaden, tranquillise.
Ant. Irritate, nettle, inflame, agitate, animate, excite, stimulate, exasperate, enrage.

Sorrow
Syn. Woe, mourning, affliction, grief, sadness, trouble.
Ant. Happiness, gladness, delight, bliss, joy.

Soul
Syn. Mind, heart, ego, clan, essence, vital, principle, genius.
Ant. Body, matter, materialisation, concreteness, embodiment.

Sound
Syn. Tone, noise, note, rational, sensible, resonance, report.
Ant. Irrational, unreasonable, silence, stillness, quietness, fallacious, impaired, broken, damaged, spoiled.

Sound
Syn. Search, test, fathom, examine.

Sour
Syn. Acid, harsh, tart, rancid.
Ant. Sweet, saccharine, honeyed, sugary.

Sour
Syn. Snappish, acrimonious peevish, surly splenetic, churlish.
Ant. Hearty, jovial, amiable, gentle, genial, lovable, cordial, benign.

Speak
Syn. Pronounce, express, say, utter, chat, announce, declare, talk, discourse, enunciate, declaim, deliver, articulate, tell.
Ant. Mum, silent, absence of sound.

Spectacle
Syn. Pageant, scene, show, sight, display, representation, exhibition.
Ant. Elude, elope, elusive, elusion.

Speech
Syn. Sermon, utterance, address, discourse, homily, speaking, talk, oratory, oration, harangue, language, lecture.
Ant. Hush, silence, speechlessness, taciturnity, stillness.

Speed
Syn. Quickness, impetuosity, haste, rapidity, swiftness, velocity.
Ant. Slowness, langour, sluggishness.

Spend
Syn. Disburse, waste, dissipate, expend, squander, exhaust.
Ant. Save, store, amass, hoard, keep, accumulate.

Spend
Syn. Bestow, lavish.
Ant. Miserliness, close-fisted.

Spirit
Syn. Mind, heart, ego, vital.
Ant. Body, matter, embodiment.

Spiteful
Syn. Rancorous, malignant, malicious.
Ant. Benign, beneficent, benevolent, benignant.

Splendid
Syn. Resplendent, radiant, brilliant, beaming, shining.
Ant. Dull, dark, dim, tarnished, cloudy.

Splendid
Syn. Superb, glorious, sumptuous, gorgeous, fine, grand.
Ant. Mean, inferior, sordid, shabby, ordinary, poor.

Spoil
Syn. Damage, corrupt, injure, mar, disfigure, vitiate.
Ant. Improve, mend, better, ameliorate.

Sport
Syn. Pastime, chase, hunting, jesting, mockery, merriment, athletics, ridicule, freak, recreation.
Ant. Activity, work, profession, business.

Stain
Syn. Blot, tint, tinge, colour, disgrace, dishonour, spoil, sully, tarnish.
Ant. Clarity, wash, clean, purify.

Stand
Syn. Pause, stay, stop, remain, keep up, endure, abide, continue.
Ant. Decline, falter, fall, fail, sink, yield, succumb.

Stamp
Syn. Impress, imprint, press, brand, mark, print.
Ant. Efface, erase, obliterate, delete, expunge.

State
Syn. Maintain, testify, swear, affirm, avow, certify, claim, depose, pronounce, say, set-forth, vouchsafe, inform, assert, propound.

Statement
Syn. Account, narration, declaration, avowal, assertion, announcement, utterance.
Ant. Refutation, disavowal, contradiction, denial, negation.

Stationary
Syn. Immobile, still, inert, fixed, quiescent, motionless, immovable.
Ant. Movable, changeable, portable, mobile.

Steady
Syn. Staunch, unwavering, steadfast.
Ant. Capricious, unreliable, fickle, irresolute.

Steady
Syn. Constant, undeviating, stable, regular, firm, consistent, uniform.
Ant. Irregular, unstable, wavering, changeable, variable, unsteady, inconstant, inconsistent.

Steal
Syn. Extract, swindle, rob, extort, filch, commit, theft, embezzle, purloin, pilfer, pillage, plunder.
Ant. Give back, refund, repay, surrender, return, restore.

Steep
Syn. High, sharp, sheer, abrupt, precipitous.
Ant. Gradual, low level, slight, easy, gentle.

Stick
Syn. Persist, cleave, hold, adhere.
Ant. Disconnect, dislodge, part, divide, move, segregate.

Stick
Syn. Attach, glue, fasten, solder, gum, fix.
Ant. Separate, detach, remove, disunite.

Stiff
Syn. Prime, frigid, severe, starchy.
Ant. Affable, cordial, gracious.

Stiff
Syn. Unbending, rigid, inflexible, unyielding.
Ant. Flexible, elastic, yielding, lithe, pliable, limber, lissom.

Still
Syn. Yet, however, nevertheless, notwithstanding.
Ant. Never, not ever, on no occasion.

Still
Syn. Motionless, calm, peaceful, serene, stagnant, quiet, stationary, pacific.
Ant. Moving, flowing, excited, disturbed, troubled, agitated, running, flustered.

Stimulate
Syn. Instigate, whet, pur, inflame, inspirit, goad, provoke, incite.
Ant. Prevent, hinder, deter, dissuade.

Stimulus
Syn. Spur, incitement, inducement, incentive.
Ant. Deterrent, hinderance.

Stop
Syn. Terminate, quit, finish, desist, end, cease, abstain, conclude, discontinue, give over, intermit.
Ant. Begin, set going, set in motion, institute, commence, enter upon, inaugurate, originate.

Storm
Syn. Tempest, bluster, rage, tornado, hurricane, blizzard.
Ant. Calmness, fair, weather, stormlessness.

Stromy
Syn. Boisterous, squally, rough, tempestuous, violent, roaring.
Ant. Quiet, silent, motionless, serene, stationary.

Story
Syn. Account, myth, record, tale, yarn, narration, novel, relation, legend.
Ant. Annals, memoir, chronicle, history, biography.

Strange
Syn. Queer, extraordinary, unique, unnatural, unusual, uncommon, odd, eccentric, inexplicable.
Ant. Normal, everyday, usual, natural, ordinary.

Stranger
Syn. Newcomer, fantastic person, eccentric, fresher, foreigner, queer.
Ant. Host, regular, comer, citizen permanent, dweller.

Stretch
Syn. Expand, extend, elongate, lengthen.
Ant. Shorten, diminish, contract, curtail, reduce, lessen.

Strict
Syn. Careful, accurate, exact, scrupulous.
Ant. Inexact, rambling, vague, loose, faulty, inaccurate indistinct.

Strict
Syn. Close, string, exacting, rigorous, harsh, stern, severe.
Ant. Clement, mild, forbearing, lenient, gentle.

Strike
Syn. Touch, clash, hit, meet, collide.
Ant. Forgotten, untouched, depart.

Strike
Syn. Smite, thump, hit, beat, knock.
Ant. Caress, hug, embrace, fondle.

Strong
Syn. Intense, glaring, brilliant, vivid, dazzling.
Ant. Pale, dull, weak, dim, indistinct, faint.

Strong
Syn. Vigorous, hardy, athletic, sturdy, muscular, forceful, forcible, powerful, potent.
Ant. Sickly, delicate, fragile, frail, unhealthy, infirm, debilitated.

Stupid
Syn. Crass, dunce, dull, dumb.
Ant. Wise, rational, intelligent, sagacious, sensible, shrewd, discerning, perspicacious.

Subject
Syn. Treat, expose, submit, conquer, subdue, vanquish, text, matter, subordinate, theme, topic.
Ant. Sovereign, chief, ruler, head, king, potentate, monarch.

Sublime
Syn. Superb, grand, lofty, majestic, noble glorious, exalted, splendid, resplendent, beautiful.
Ant. Mean, base, ridiculous, insignificant, little, petty.

Subsidy
Syn. Tribute, aid, gift, grant, pension, support, subvention, reward, premium, allowance, bonus, appropriation, indemnity.

Substantial
Syn. Actual, material, tangible, palpable, perceptible, corporeal, real, existing.
Ant. Illusive, unsubstantial, illusory, unreal, chimerical, shadowy, fanciful, fancied.

Substitute
Syn. Exchange, duplicate, depute, equivalent, make-shift, representative, proxy, deputy, agent, delegate, achieve, thrive, win, attain, flourish, prevail, prosper.
Ant. Lose, be defeated, miss, miscarry, come short, fail, fall short.

Success
Syn. Successfulness, run of luck, proficiency, stroke, half the battle, prize, upper hand, whip hand, mastery, advantage.
Ant. Failure, breakdown, collapse, miscarriage, fiasco, failing.

Successful
Syn. Prosperous, felicitous, fortunate, lucky.
Ant. Disastrous, unfortunate, ill-omened, ill-starred, luckless, calamitous, ill-fated.

Sudden
Syn. Momentary, brief, rapid, quick, unexpected, rash, unanticipated, unforeseen.
Ant. Awaited, gradual, anticipated, progressive.

Suffer
Syn. Brook, allow, permit, admit.
Ant. Refuse, debar, ban, forbid, repudiate, veto.

Suffer
Syn. Bear, sustain, tolerate, endure, pass through.
Ant. Refuse, withstand, repeal, resist, thwart, rebuff.

Suitable
Syn. Appropriate, eligible, pertinent, relevant, fitting, seemly, convenient, becoming.
Ant. Unsuitable, inappropriate, irrelevant, unfitting, unseemly, untimely, improper.

Summary
Syn. Epitome, outline, precis, synopsis, abridgement, digest.
Ant. Amplification, extension, expansion, development, enlargement.

Superficial
Syn. External, shallow, slight, outward outer.
Ant. Penetrating, deep, thorough, profound.

Superior
Syn. Excellent, major, triumphant, leading, grand, great, preponderant, first-rate, pre-eminent.
Ant. Inferior, mean fellow, worm, tiny, small, unimportant, good-for-nothing creature.

Supply
Syn. Furnish, bestow, yield, present, contribute.
Ant. Dissipate, assimilate, exhaust, devour, consume.

Support

Syn. Prop, stay, maintenance, living, sustenance, assistance, patronage, aid, help, influence, bear, cherish, hold up, keep up, maintain, uphold, carry.

Ant. Throw down, overthrow, destroy, drop, abandon, betra break down, cast down, demolish, desert.

Suppose

Syn. Guess, think, surmise, imagine, deem conjecture.

Ant. Know, be sure, conclude, ascertain, discover.

Suppress

Syn. Subdue, overpower, bridle, quash, restrain, quell, check, moderate, repress, impede.

Ant. Inflame, rout, egg, excite, provoke, agitate, kindle.

Surprising

Syn. Staggering, unexpected, marvellous, startling, striking, astonishing, amazing.

Ant. Everyday, ordinary, usual, normal, customary, habitual, expected, wanted, common.

Surrender

Syn. Leave, resign, yield, waive, let go, leave, give up, give over, cede, alienate, abandon.

Ant. Withhold, hold, reserve, suppress, retain, detain.

Suspend

Syn. Debar, stay, hinder, stop, withhold, interrupt, discontinue fall, defer, delay.

Ant. Begin, keep on, keep up, urge on, protract, continue, expedite, prolong.

Suspicion

Syn. Mistrust, distrust, misgiving.

Ant. Trust, confidence, faith.

Suspicious

Syn. Unbelieving, doubtful, mistrustful, questionable.

Ant. Trustful, trustworthy, straight, straightforward, honourable, honest.

Sweet
Syn. Mild, gentle, lovable, tender, attractive.
Ant. Crabbed, testy, snappish, petulant, splenetic, sour, surly, cross, touchy.

Sweet
Syn. Saccharine, honeyed, sugary.
Ant. Bitter, acerose, acrid, sharp.

Sweet
Syn. Wholesome, clean, balm, pure, fresh.
Ant. Stale, stinking, foul, decomposed, offensive, putrid, rotten.

Sweetness
Syn. Sugariness, sugary, confection, drops, jujube, kindness.
Ant. Sourness, tasteness, flatness.

Swell
Syn. Distend, heave, mangify, bungle, enhance, amplify, dilate.
Ant. Shorten, contract, reduce, decrease, diminish, abridge, attenuate.

Sympathy
Syn. Kindness, love, fellow-feeling, compassion, agreement, understanding, accord.
Ant. Pitilessness, cruetly, hard-heartedness, selfishness.

Synonymos
Syn. Like, similar, synonymic, same, equivalent, identical, alike, corresponding.
Ant. Antonyms, different, opposite, contradictory.

System
Syn. manner, mode, rule, regularity, method, order.
Ant. Disarrangement, confusion, chaos, irregularity.

Systematic
Syn. Methodical, regular, orderly.
Ant. Irregular, casual, fortuitous, unmethodical, occasional.

Tact
Syn. Finesse, discretion, skill, cleverness, consideration.
Ant. Discourtesy, frankness, roughness, bluntless, simplicity.

Take
Syn. Accept, receive, get.
Ant. Reject, spurn, repudiate, refuse, decline, discard.

Take
Syn. Clasp, seize, grasp, capture.
Ant. Give, hand over, pay, deliver.

Talent
Syn. Ability, knack, genius, aptitude, skill.
Ant. Unskilfulness, idleness, stupidity, inefficiency.

Taste
Syn. Polish, culture, virtue, tastefulness, delicacy, discrimination, savour, finesse.
Ant. Impoliteness, tastelessness, vulgarity.

Tasty
Syn. Refined, smart.
Ant. Gaudy, vulgar, ostentatious.

Tasty
Syn. Appetising, luscious, delicious, palatable.
Ant. Nasty, sickening nauseous, flavourless, insipid.

Tax
Syn. Assessment, impost, tariff, tribute, tithe, levy, exaction, excise, customs, rate, toll.

Teachable
Syn. Docile, complain, tractable.
Ant. Intractable, contumacious, unmanageble, disobedient.

Teacher

Syn. Professor, schoolmaster, master, instructor, lecturer, preceptor.

Ant. Student, pupil, disciple, learner.

Teaching

Syn. Instruction, education, tutorship, direction, guidance, practice, sermon, indoctrination, droll, exercise.

Ant. Learn, acquire, skill, go to school, be instructed, read.

Tear

Syn. Lanciniate, split, lacerate, part, sever, rupture.

Ant. Repair, patch, rectify, restore, mend.

Tearful

Syn. Weeping, mournful.

Ant. Joyous, happy.

Tease

Syn. Irritate, chafe, provoke, vex, plague, torment, annoy.

Ant. Hush, compose, conciliate, appease, calm, soothe, mollify.

Tell

Syn. Communicate, narrate, divulge, inform, disclose, reveal, acquaint, inform, relate, apprise, communicate.

Ant. Conceal, dissemble, hide, smother, stifle, suppress, repress.

Temerity

Syn. Hastiness, rashness, recklessness, presumption, hardihood.

Ant. Overconfidence, impetuosity, precipitation, recklessness, venturesomeness, audacity.

Temperance

Syn. Forbearance, self-denial, renunciation, moderation, abnegation, sobriety, soberness, asceticism.

Ant. Extremeness, indulgence, luxury, intoxication.

Temporary

Syn. Evanescent, ephemeral, brief, momentary, fleeting, transitory, transient.

Ant. Permanent, perpetual, immutable, constant, lasting, stable, changeless, imperishable.

Tempt

Syn. Seduce, decoy, inveigle, entice, wheedle.

Ant. Deter, disincline, discourage, care, restraint, dissuade.

Temptation

Syn. Enticement, attraction, allurement, charm, fascination, bait.

Ant. Repulsion, turning away, contempt, avoidance, hatred.

Tendency

Syn. Proneness, trend, bias, leaning, proclivity, propensity.

Ant. Aversion, distaste, dislike, disinclination, antipathy, detestation.

Term

Syn. Article, name, word, phrase, member, denomination, condition, expression.

Ant. Unconditional, liberal, lenient, relaxing.

Terse

Syn. Neat, short, succinct, laconic, compact, compendious, summary, sententious, condensed.

Ant. Diffuse, verbose, prolix, lengthy, wordy.

Test

Syn. Ordeal, examination, assay, experiment, criterion, standard, prove, try.

Testimony

Syn. Attestation, evidence, witness, proof, affirmation, deposition, certification.

Thankful

Syn. Obliged, beholden, grateful.

Ant. Thankless, ungrateful.

Theory

Syn. Belief, postulate, assumption, speculation, doctrine, conjecture, hyphothesis, supposition.

Ant. Practice.

Thick

Syn. Confused, hoarse, guttural, inarticulate, indistinct.

Ant. Distinct.

Thick
Syn. Fat, condensed, solid, dense.
Ant. Liquid, rarefied, thin.

Thick
Syn. Obscure, dirty, muddy.
Ant. Clear, limpid.

Thin
Syn. Diluted, flimsy, scanty, poor, sparse, attenuated.
Ant. Strong, solid, wholesome, sturdy.

Thin
Syn. Lean, gaunt, slim, skinny, scraggy, slender, slight.
Ant. Obese, fat, corpulent, stout.

Thing
Syn. Article, object, being, body, something, entity.
Ant. Nothing, cipher, nought.

Though
Syn. Assuming, if, although, allowing, nevertheless, granting.
AAnt. Factural, practical, bar, ban.

Thought
Syn. Meditation, rumination, consideration, deliberation, musing, reflection, thinking.
Ant. Act, fact, practice, perform, operate.

Thought
Syn. View, conception, belief, idea, intention.
Ant. Misconception.

Thoughtful
Syn. Attentive, circumspect, heedful, provident, prudent, careful, considerate, mindful.
Ant. Careless, gay, remiss, reckless, negligent, neglectful, inconsiderate, inattentive, giddy.

Threaten
Syn. Denounce, intimidate.
Ant. Reassure.

Threaten
Syn. Portend, warn, forebode.

Throng
Syn. Jam, host, mass, multitude, crowd.

Through
Syn. During, among, within.
Ant. Finish, end, concluded.

Tie
Syn. Knit, connect, unite, joint, fasten, fetter.
Ant. Disconnect, disunite, unlock, unfetter, unfasten, loosen, unbind.

Tight
Syn. Taut, stretched, tense.
Ant. Loose, slack.

Tight
Syn. Narrow, close, compact.
Ant. Open.

Time
Syn. Age, date, duration, era, sequence, while, term, succession, season, period, epoch.
Ant. Eternity.

Timely
Syn. Prompt, early, seasonable, opportune.
Ant. Tardy, unseasonable, late, inopportune.

Timid
Syn. Bashful, coy, shy, modest, retiring.
Ant. Forward, confident.

Timid
Syn. Afraid, fearful, faint-hearted, pusillanimous.
Ant. Bold, unafraid, daring, brave.

Tip
Syn. Cant, dip, tilt, slope, list, slant, lean, incline, heel, cover.
Ant. Base, bottom, foot.

Tire
Syn. Fatigue, harass, were out, weary, fag, exhaust, jade.
Ant. Invigorate, recreate, repose, rest, refresh, relieve.

Together
Syn. Concurrently, conjointly, simultaneously, unitedly.
Ant. Separately, individually, independently, unconnectedly.

Toleration
Syn. Tolerance, temperance, endurance, laxity, forgiveness, clemency, moderation, sufferance.
Ant. Bigotry, authoritarianism, dogmatism, fanaticism.

Tongue
Syn. Parlance, vernacular, language, speech, idiom.

Tool
Syn. Weapon, utensil, mechanism, instrument, implement, appliance, apparatus.

Top
Syn. Pinnacle, culmination, apex, summit, crest, head, crown, zenith.
Ant. Base, floor, foundation, foot, bottom, ground.

Topic
Syn. Issue, question, theme, division, head, matter, motion, proposition, subject, point.

Torture
Syn. Anguish, pain, agony, torment, distress, persecute.
Ant. Allay, soothe, relief, comfort, palliate, ease, relieve, deaden, lessen.

Total
Syn. Whole, entire, aggregate, gross, complete.
Ant. Part, segment, division, portion, proportion, component, constituent.

Touch
Syn. Graze, handle, move.

Touch
Syn. Impress, affect, feel.

Tough
Syn. Difficult, hard.
Ant. Easy, simple.

Tough
Syn. Fibrous, rough, durable, strong, firm, tenacious, rigid.
Ant. Soft, tender, feeble, frail, weak, delicate.

Trace
Syn. Footmark, sign, remnant, track, trail, vestige, memorial footstep, remains, impression.

Trade
Syn. Occupation, profession, business, vocation, calling, pursuit.

Tragedy
Syn. Misforture, disaster, affliction, adversity, calamity, catastrophe.
Ant. Farce, comedy, humour, drama.

Train
Syn. Discipline, school, drill, educate, instruct.
Ant. Raw, untrained, fresh, illiterate.

Trained
Syn. Proficient, qualified, practised, expert, efficient.
Ant. Untrained, unqualified, inexperienced, clumsy, inexpert, unskilled, inefficient.

Transact
Syn. Treat, perform, carry on, do, negotiate, accomplish, act, conduct.
Ant. Mishandle, mismanage, misconduct.

Transaction
Syn. Business, act, proceeding, deed, action, affair, doing.

Transient
Syn. Brief, fleeting, fugitive, short, transitory, livid, momentary, fitting, flying, passing, evanescent, temporary.
Ant. Presistent, perpetual, unfading immortal, lasting, eternal, abiding.

Transfer
Syn. Transmit, exchange, transplant, convey, assign, remove, make over, transplant.
Ant. Place, secure, fix, plant, settle, establish.

Transform
Syn. Metamorphose, translate, change, transfigure, convert.
Ant. Immortalise, perserve, prepetuate, eternalise.

Trap
Syn. Net, snare, ambush, catch, enslave, artifice, gin, stratagem.

Travel
Syn. Travelling, expedition, wayfaring, trip, crossing, globetrotting, airing, circuit, itinerary, journey.
Ant. Idleness, inertia, staying at home, stationariness.

Treacherous
Syn. Traitorous, disloyal, unfaithful, unreliable, untrustworthy, perfidious.
Ant. Faithful, loyal, trusty, devoted, reliable, trustworthy.

Treachery
Syn. Perfidy, falsity, deception, disloyalty, infidelity.
Ant. Faithfulness, fidelity, firmness, loyalty.

Tremble
Syn. Vibrate, shudder, quake, oscillate, quiver.
Ant. Stiffen, gell, petrify.

Trembling
Syn. Vibrating, rocking, oscillating, tremulous, shaking.
Ant. Steady, still, unwavering, motionless, firm stationary, immobile, stable.

Trial
Syn. Attempt, endeavour, Test, experiment, proof, examination, Trouble, hardship, action, suit, grief, ordeal, suffering, hearing, distress.
Ant. Unattended, untouched, untreated.

Trick
Syn. Wile, skill, ruse, guile, imposture, invention, cunning.
Ant. Artlessness, ingeniousness, innocence, openness, guilelessness, honesty, fairness, frankness, truth, sincerity.

Trifle
Syn. Toy, gewgaw, idle, dally, play, bauble.
Ant. Treasure, valuables, gem.

True

Syn. Truthful, veracious, faithful, accurate, loyal, staunch, genuine, honest, real, trustworthy, constant, veritable.

Ant. Disloyal, inaccurate, wrong, erroneous, faulty, treacherous, unfaithful, untrustworthy, fictitious, deceiving, misleading.

Truly

Syn. Veritably, positively, faithfully, actually, sincerely, truthfully, really, unquestionably.

Ant. Untruly, falsely, doubtfully, deceivingly, uncertainly, incorrectly, questionably.

Trust

Syn. Reliance, confidence, keeping, credit, office, duty, expectation, hope, credence, belief.

Ant. Distrust, faithlessness, breaking of pledge, deception.

Trust

Syn. Rely on, depend on, confide in, believe.

Ant. Doubt, mistrust, suspect.

Truth

Syn. Integrity, frankness, straightforwardness, fealty, sincerity, fidelity, faith, faithfulness, probity.

Ant. Deception, guile, chicanery, imposture, duplicity, deceit, deceitfulness.

Truth

Syn. Verity, reality, correctness, veracity, precision.

Ant. Falsehood, fabrication, lie, mendacity.

Try

Syn. Endeavour, essay, strive, undertake, attempt.

Ant. Abandon, dismiss, throw away, drop, give up, throw up, pass by, overlook, neglect.

Tune

Syn. Rotation, cycle, air, melody.

Ant. Disharmony, dissonance, discordance, discord.

Turn

Syn. Deflection, twist, deviation, change, bend, alteration, variation.

Ant. Directness, straightness, rectilinearity.

141

Turn

Syn. Twirl, revolve, spin, reverse, invert, transform, convert, metamorphose, defect, grow, become, dependent, hang, rest, away.

Ant. Stabilise, continue, staighten, conserve, maintain, perpetuate.

Typical

Syn. Indicative, symbolical, regular, illustrative, normal.

Ant. Abnormal, singular, divergent, peculiar.

Tyranny

Syn. Totalitarianism, autocracy, oppression, depotism, rigour, harshness.

Ant. Pity, love, compassion, softness, sympathy.

Tyrant

Syn. Persecutor, autocrat, oppressor, bully, despot.

Ant. Subject, subordinate, victim.

Ugly
Syn. Unsightly, ungainly, ghastly, uncomely, horrible, uncouth, deformed, hideous, loathsome, monstrous, unlovely.

Ant. Gracious, pretty, attractive, beautiful, good looking, seemly, comely, handsome.

Unalterable
Syn. Changeless, unchangeable, variable, immutable, permanent, constant.

Ant. Changeable, revocable, mutable, variable, inconstant, alterable.

Unanimity
Syn. Harmony, unison, agreement, accord, concord.

Ant. Disagreement contention, difference, variance, disharmony.

Unanimous
Syn. Agreeing, concordant, united.

Ant. Discordant, deviating, disagreeing, differing.

Unanswerable
Syn. Certain, infallible, conclusive, incontrovertible, irrefutable, undeniable.

Ant. Disputable, fallible, refutable, inconclusive, weak.

Uncertain
Syn. Fluctuating, inconstant, fitful, capricious, irregular, unreliable, changeable, precarious.

Ant. Reliable, stable, trustworthy, unchangeable, regular, steady, permanent.

Uncertain
Syn. Indefinite, questionable, unsettled, dubious, equivocal, doubtful.

Ant. Certain, definite, indisputable, incontestable, unquestionable, undeniable, positive.

Unclean
Syn. Impure, squalid, dirty, foul, sullied.
Ant. Pure, unsoiled, unsullied, clean, immaculate.

Unconcerned
Syn. Nonchalant, apathetic, cool, disinterested, indifferent.
Ant. Solicitous, interested, concerned, anxious.

Unconquerable
Syn. Insuperable, invincible, indomitable, insurmountable.
Ant. Weak, powerless, feeble, conquerable.

Under
Syn. Lower, subordinate, inferior, below, underneath, beneath.
Ant. Overhead, above, over.

Understand
Syn. comprehend, realise, apprehend, discern, preceive, grasp.
Ant. Misunderstand, misinterpret, misconceive.

Undertake
Syn. Guarantee, promise, engage, stipulate, agree.
Ant. Free, independent, unconditional.

Undertake
Syn. Enter upon, engage in.
Ant. Overtake, avoid, escape.

Undertaking
Syn. Contract, endeavour, trade, tall, orders, enterpirse, promise, engagement, venture.
Ant. Irresponsibility, refusal, truancy, escapade, avoidance.

Uneasy
Syn. Restless, restive, unquiet, disturbed, awkward, uncomfortable.
Ant. Content, undisturbed, restful, statisfied, comfortable, quiet, contented.

Unfair
Syn. Unjust, inequitable, partial, dishonest, wrongful, dishonourable, biased.
Ant. Fair, just, honest, unprejudiced, neutral, impartial, equitable, unbiased.

Unfaithful

Syn. Unreliable, disloyal faithless, treacherous, inconstant.

Ant. Faithful, staunch, reliable, trustworthy, loyal.

Unfit

Syn. Inappropriate, unqualified, inapt, incapable, improper unsuitable.

Ant. Suitable, pertinent, relevant, proper, fit, appropriate.

Unfortunate

Syn. Frustrated, luckless, deplorable, infelicitous, calamitous, unlucky.

Ant. Auspicious, lucky, favourable, happy, fortunate.

Unhappiness

Syn. Wrechedness, distress, sorrow, woe, misery.

Ant. Happiness, bliss, gaiety, blessedness, cheerfulness.

Unhappy

Syn. Unlucky, unfortunate, calamitous, disastrous.

Ant. Favourable, fortunate, lucky.

Unhappy

Syn. Disconsolate, distressed, afflicted, miserable, sorrowful.

Ant. Blithe gay, jovial, hilarious, joyous, cheerful.

Unholy

Syn. Wicked, sinful, irreligious, profane, unrighteous, depraved.

Ant. Holy, devine, religious, morel.

Union

Syn. Coalition, concert, unity, juncture, junction, cooperation, combination, unification, oneness.

Ant. Divorce, division, analysis, contrairity, disassociation, separation, disconnection, schism.

Unite

Syn. Adjoin, join, conjoin, concerhtrate, connect, affix, append, associate, combine.

Ant. Detach, diconnect, disjoin, disassociate, separate.

Universal

Syn. All-embracing, international, complete, general, whole, comprehensive, entire.

Ant. Parochial, sectarian, partisan, sectional, factionary.

Unlucky
Syn. Disastrous, ill-starred, ill-fated, fatal, calamitous,
Ant. Lucky, auspicious, fortunate.

Untidy
Syn. Slatternly, disorderly, sluggish, careless, slovenly, unkempt.
Ant. Neat, clean, smart, immaculate, tidy, shapely, trim.

Unusual
Syn. Extraordinary, remarkable, peculiar, uncommon, queer, exceptional, rare, singular.
Ant. Usual, common, hackneyed, habitual, commonplace, everyday, ordinary.

Unwilling
Syn. Loath, disinclined, reluctant, indisposed.
Ant. Willing, eager, disposed, ardent, keen, anxious.

Urge
Syn. Stimulate, spur, incite, force, drive, impel.
Ant. Deter, discourage, disincline, warn, disposed.

Urgent
Syn. Critical, pressing, important, insistent, imperative.
Ant. Minor, inconsiderable, unimportant, trifling, insignificant, petty, trivial.

Use
Syn. Employ, appliance, avail, practise, utility, utilisation, application, consumption, employment, exercise.
Ant. Uselessness, disuse, loss, abuse, dumping, misuse, unemployment.

Useful
Syn. Serviceable, beneficial, advantageous, helpful, profitable, valuable.
Ant. Useless, unprofitable, unhelpful, unfruitful.

Unless
Syn. Wothless, unprofitable, unserviceable, profitless, abortive.
Ant. Unhelpful, unfruitful.

Usual
Syn. Familiar, wonted, public, prevalent, habitual, everyday, common, customary, frequent, general, infrequent.

Ant. Specific, unusual, unparalleled.

Utility
Syn. Service, use, advantage, profit, policy, benefit, avail, usefulness, serviceableness.

Ant. Disadvantage, unprofitableness, worthlessness, uselessness, impolity, folly, unutility.

V

Vacant

Syn. Unoccupied, waste, vacuous, unfilled, leisure, blank, empty, devoid, unemployed, untenanted.

Ant. Occupied, jammed, replete, packed, filled, full, brimmed, brimful, brimming, busy, crammed, gorged.

Vain

Syn. Futile, idle, inconstant, trifling, trivial, unsatisfying, worthless, valueless, vapid, visionary, unserviceable, delusive, fruitless, deceitful, empty, shadowy.

Ant. Adequate, valid, useful, advantageous, profitable, real, serviceable, efficient, solid, sound, competent, effective.

Valid

Syn. Binding, defensible, powerful, efficacious, cogent, logical.

Ant. Invalid, unconvincing, unsound, lame, feeble, weak, illogical.

Valuable

Syn. Estimate, worthy.

Ant. Worthless, cheap, useless.

Valuable

Syn. Expensive, precious, costly.

Ant. Worthless, cheap, valueless, base.

Value

Syn. Estimate, appraise, assess.

Ant. Un-estimated, priceless.

Value

Syn. Appreciate, treasure, prize.

Ant. Belittle, decry, under-rate, under-value, disparage, depreciate.

Vanish

Syn. Dissolve, depart, suddenly fade away, disappear.

Ant. Appear, arrive, emerge.

Vanity
Syn. Pride, egotism, arrogance, conceit.
Ant. Unobtrusiveness, meekness, modesty.

Variety
Syn. Variation, difference, many-sidedness, assortment.
Ant. Recurrence, repetitiveness, sameness, dullness.

Various
Syn. Different, multitudinous, numerous, variegated, sundry, manifold, many, several, multiform.
Ant. Identical, few.

Verbal
Syn. Spoken, oral, unwritten.
Ant. Inscribed, printed, recorded, written.

Versatile
Syn. Expert, clever.
Ant. Dullness, stupid.

Versatile
Syn. Volatile, capricious, mercurial, constant, unsteady, changeable.
Ant. Steady, constant, invariable, unchangeable, undeviating, unwavering, permanent.

Vertical
Syn. Erect, perpendicular, upright.
Ant. Horizontal, inclining, oblique, slanting, sloping.

Very
Syn. Exceedingly, highly, extremely, exceptionally, excessively.
Ant. Sameness, lowly, smooth.

Vibrate
Syn. Quiver, shiver, swing, sway.
Ant. Congeal, gell, solidify.

Victory
Syn. Triumph, supremacy, success, achievement, ascendancy, conquest, mastery.
Ant. Rout, disaster, defeat, miscarriage, failure, disappointment, overthrow, retreat.

View
Syn. Vista, outlook, scenery, panorama, prospect, seascape, landscape.
Ant. Insight, internal, meditation.

View
Syn. Judgement, idea, notion, theory.
Ant. Misconception, misunderstanding, misapprehension.

View
Syn. Purpose, end, design, meaning, object.
Ant. Beginning, original-self, undesigned.

View
Syn. Watch, behold, inspect, eye, scan, see, contemplate.
Ant. Ignore, neglect, disgregard.

Vigilant
Syn. Alert, wide-awake, wakeful, cautious, on the look out, wary, watchful, circumspect.
Ant. Careless, neglectful, unwary, heedless, inattentive, uncautious, inconsiderable, negligent.

Violation
Syn. Trespass, infraction, infringement, transgression.
Ant. Compliance, adherence, concurrence, observance, acquiescence.

Violent
Syn. Wild, sharp, server, acute, fierce, frantic, intense, mad, raging, raving, tumultous, turbulent, infuriate, immoderate, impetuous.
Ant. Quiet, cool, collected, frigid, peaceful, unruffled, placid.

Virtue
Syn. Chastity, worth, worthiness, rightness, justice, honour, honestly, probity, truth, uprightness, rectitude, faithfulness, duty.
Ant. Wrong, wickedness, sin, depravity, viciousness, evil, vice, failing, corruption.

Vision
Syn. Phantom, chimera, hallucination, apparition, illusion, ghost, mirage, spectre, delusion.

Vision
Syn. Sight, seeing.
Ant. Sightlessness, blindness.

Visitor
Syn. Guest, caller, company.
Ant. Host.

Vital
Syn. Alive, animate, living, indispensable, necessary, important, essential.
Ant. Immaterial, dead, trifling, lifeless, inert, unimportant, insignificant.

Vivid
Syn. Brilliant, glaring, bright, telling, graphic, expressive.
Ant. Dim, dull, tarnished.

Voice
Syn. Utterance, address, talk, speaking.
Ant. Hush, silence, speechlessness, stillness.

Volume
Syn. Capacity, dimensions, contents, bulk.
Ant. Disability, unlimited.

Volume
Syn. Tone, work, book.
Ant. Untonned, disharmonious.

Voluntary
Syn. Gratuitous, discretional, willing, unconstrained, optional, spontaneous.
Ant. Enforced, imperative, compulsory.

Volunteer
Syn. Undertake, offer, proffer, tend, propose.
Ant. Refuse, repudiate, veto, decline.

Vulgar
Syn. Ordinary, native, common, vernacular.
Ant. Exotic, extraneous, acquired.

Vulgar
Syn. Coarse, unrefined, gross, base, rude.
Ant. Refined, polished, tylish, gentlemanly, courteous, genteel.

Wages
Syn. Payment, hire, compensation, remuneration, salary, reward.
Ant. Rewardlessness, unproductivity, fruitlessness, waste.

Wait
Syn. Half, stop, await, remain.
Ant. Press, move, urge.

Wait
Syn. Serve, minister, attend.

Wakeful
Syn. Active, vigilant, awake, watchful.
Ant. Asleep, sleeping, slumbering, inactive, quiescent, lethargic.

Walk
Syn. Stroll, hike, tramp, ramble, saunter.
Ant. Hasten, run, hurry, race, sprint.

Wander
Syn. Depart, roam, digress, ramble, range, deviate.
Ant. Abide, rest, settle.

Want
Syn. Proverty, need, deficiency, shortage, absence, omission, missing, desire, craving, inadequacy.
Ant. Sufficiency, desirelessness, fulfilment, satisfaction, wealth.

Want
Syn. Wish for, crave, covet, desire.

War
Syn. Contention, discord, battle, hostility, strife.
Ant. Peace, calm, harmony, concord, agreement.

Wash
Syn. Lave, clean, cleanse, rinse.
Ant. Soil, pollute, dirty, contaminate, besmirch, defile, begrime.

Washing
Syn. Ablution, bathing, cleansing, purification, lavation, cleaning, bath.
Ant. Taint, staining stain, contamination, pollution, defiling, defilement, soiling, soil, befouling.

Wasteful
Syn. Prodigal, thriftless, lavish, improvident, imprudent, unthrifty, reckless.
Ant. Sparing, miserly, economical, prudent, frugal, provident.

Wavering
Syn. Oscillating, unsteady, fluctuating, undecided, undetermined, inconstant, vacillating, faltering, quivering.
Ant. Steady, unwavering, determined, firm, resolute, unhesitating, steadfast.

Weak
Syn. Unconvincing, poor, illogical, ineffectual.
Ant. Logical, rational, valid, sane, sensible, convincing.

Weak
Syn. Sickly, enervated, debilitated, fragile, feeble, frail.
Ant. Vigorous, strong, stalwart, mighty, athletic, lusty, brawny, powerful.

Weaken
Syn. Attenuate, enfeeble, sap, impair, debilitate, unnerve.
Ant. Strengthen, fortify, brace, harden.

Weakness
Syn. Lassitude, infirmity, debility, langour, frailty.
Ant. Strength, might, energy, vigour.

Weakness
Syn. Defect, fault, failing.

Wealth

Syn. Abundance, substance, riches, profusion, money, pelf, plenty, prosperity, property, possessions.

Ant. Poverty, destitution, privation, strait, distress, want, impecuniosity, insufficiency.

Wedding

Syn. Wedlock, marriage, nuptial.

Ant. Divorce, separation.

Weight

Syn. Responsibility, heaviness, pressure, load.

Ant. Lightness.

Weight

Syn. Consequence, significance, gravity, moment, importance.

Ant. Triviality, unimportance, insignificance.

Welcome

Syn. Reception, greeting, salutation, meeting, cordial, handshake.

Ant. Adieu, parting, goodbye, leave-taking, departure, godspeed.

Welcome

Syn. Hail, receive, salute, greet.

Ant. Insult, offend, abuse.

Wet

Syn. Drenched, damp, humid, rainy, showery, moisture, soak.

Ant. Dry, arid, parch, parched, dehydrate.

Whiten

Syn. Etiolate, bleach, blanch.

Ant. Darken, blacken, smudge.

Wholly

Syn. Entirely, utterly, absolutely, perfectly, completely, totally, fully.

Ant. Incompletely, partly, partially.

Wicked

Syn. Iniquitous, criminal, vile, villainous, corrupt, evil, immoral, bad, heinous, sinful.

Ant. Virtuous, incorrupt, chaste, moral, upright.

Wide
Syn. Epansive, spacious, large, broad, extensive.
Ant. Narrow, cramped, confined, circumscribed, close, limited, small.

Will
Syn. Wish, volition, resolution, decision, desire, determination, inclination.
Ant. Unwillingness, neutral, indifferent, impartial

Willingly
Syn. Voluntarily, gladly, with pleasure, freely, readily.
Ant. Unwillingly, reluctantly.

Win
Syn. Acquire, persuade, procure, gain, attain, obtain, influence, away, get, achieve.
Ant. Lose, fail.

Winding
Syn. Twisting, tortuous, serpentine, bending, curving, sinuous, meandering.
Ant. Direct, straight, underviating.

Wisdom
Syn. Knowledge, intelligence, discretion, sense, learning, erudition, discernment, sagacity, prudence.
Ant. Stupidity, ignorance, silliness.

Wise
Syn. Sensible, discreet, prudent, judicious, intelligent, sapient, sagacious.
Ant. Senseless, indiscreet, irrational, absurd, dull, stupid, silly.

Wonder
Syn. Wonderment, marvel, amazement, sensation, electrification, bewilder, amazedness, miraculousness.
Ant. Expectation, principle, castle in the air, theory, result.

Wood
Syn. Woodland, copse, jungle, thicket, grove.
Ant. City, town.

Word
Syn. Expression, term, pledge, promise, assurance.
Ant. Idea, thought, supposition.

Work
Syn. Grind, toil, product, production, deed, action, doing, employment, labour, drudgery, exertion, business.
Ant. Leisure, recreation, relaxation, repose, idleness, ease.

Workman
Syn. Mechanic, toiler, craftsman, employee, labourer.
Ant. Controller, superintendent, manager, master.

World
Syn. Globe, earth, creation.

Worship
Syn. Idolisation, reverence, veneration, homage.
Ant. Contempt, disdain, scorn, derision.

Worthless
Syn. Cheap, base, degraded, valueless, dissolute, despicable, paltry, contemptible.
Ant. Excellent, good, transcendent, estimable, costly, valuable, admirable.

Writer
Syn. Amanuensis, copyist, author, secretary, scribe.

Wrongful
Syn. Unfair, dishonest, iniquitous, unjust.
Ant. Fair, just, honest.

Xanthous
Syn. Light-skinned, golden-haired, yellow-haired, fair-haired, blonde, fair.
Ant. Brown, black, wheatish, skinned.

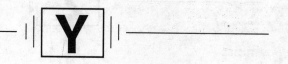

Yawn
Syn. Gape, open, wide, part, split.
Ant. Close, shut, abridge, shorten, peephole.

Yearly
Syn. Annually, per annum.

Yearn
Syn. Hanker, long, wish, desire.
Ant. Get, hope for, secure, expect.

Yeoman
Syn. Commander, petty officer, beef-eater, retainer.
Ant. Lord, governor, officer, landlord, boss.

Yield
Syn. Give way, submit, accede, waive, surrender, renounce, abandon forgo, crop, product, return.
Ant. Resist, withstand, refuse, keep back, withhold, reserve, restrain, veto, oppose, assail, contend, confront.

Yes

Syn.   Indeed, of course, yea, aye, truly, agreed, surely, certainly.
Ant.   Nay, negative, not agreed, nil, never.

Young

Syn.   Youthful, boyish, new, fresh, childish, recent.
Ant.   Old, antiquated, elderly, matured, ancient.

Youthful

Syn.   Green, early, boyish, young, childish, immature.
Ant.   Mature, elderly, aged, ripe, late, fully.

Zeal

Syn.   Zest, dedication, eagerness, devotion, earnestness, warmth, energy.
Ant.   Coolness, weakness, laziness, carelessness, apathy.

Zenith

Syn.   Summit, crown, climax, apex, top, height, acme, culmination.
Ant.   Base, zero, nullify, foundation, foot, bottom floor, gound.

Zero

Syn.   Cipher, nothing, nil.
Ant.   Zenith, acme, culmination climax.

Zone

Syn.   Tract, circumference, region, girdle, circuit.